11+ Practice Paper

Set A: Paper 1
Verbal Skills

For the GL Buckinghamshire Transfer Test

Read the following:

Do not open this booklet or start the test until you are told to do so.

1. This is a multiple-choice test. You will have around one hour to complete this paper, including the practice questions and reading time.

2. There are 2 sections in this test — English and Verbal Reasoning.
   You will have 25 minutes to complete the first section, which contains 30 questions.
   You will have 20 minutes to complete the second section, which contains 25 questions.

3. Each section starts with some examples showing you how to answer the questions.
   For each section, you will have 5 minutes to read the examples and answer some practice questions.

4. You should mark your answer to each question in pencil on the separate answer sheet.

5. Unless told otherwise, you should only mark one answer for each question.
   To mark your answer, draw a straight line through the rectangle next to the option you have chosen. If you make a mistake, rub it out and mark your new answer clearly.

6. Make sure you keep your place on the answer sheet and mark your answer in the box that has the same number as the question.

7. Do as many questions as you can. If you get stuck on a question, choose the answer that you think is most likely to be correct, then move on to the next question.

8. You should do any rough working on a separate piece of paper.

Work carefully, but go as quickly as you can.

Exam set ELPCE3

Section 1: English

Example and Practice Questions

You have **5 minutes** to complete practice questions P1 to P3. Read each example carefully before attempting to answer the practice question.

The Burj Khalifa

For many centuries, the world's tallest buildings were grand European churches. However, the early 20th century saw a new contender — the skyscraper. Since 1998, Malaysia and Taiwan have successively laid claim to the world's tallest skyscraper, a record formerly held exclusively by the USA. There is also a skyscraper being planned
5 in Kuwait which could one day take that title. However, perhaps the most imposing skyscraper right now is the impressive Burj Khalifa in the UAE in western Asia.
   The Burj Khalifa is a mixed-purpose tower that has officially held the record for the tallest building on earth since 2009. Built over five years using more than 4,000 tonnes of steel, this imposing tower is glazed almost entirely in crystal-clear windows reinforced
10 with silicone and aluminium. It looms over the city of Dubai, reaching a stunning height of 828 metres. The concrete foundations and first 100 floors of the structure were finished in just under three years.

Answer these questions about the text. You can refer back to the text if you need to.
Pick the best answer and mark its letter on your answer sheet.

Example

According to the text, which of these countries has not been home to the world's tallest skyscraper?

A Kuwait
B UAE
C Taiwan
D USA
E Malaysia

Answer

A *Kuwait is the only country not mentioned as being home to the world's tallest skyscraper at some point in time.*

Try the practice question below.

P1 Which of these materials is not an essential part of the Burj Khalifa's structure?

A Steel
B Glass
C Concrete
D Crystal
E Aluminium

The sentences below contain some spelling mistakes. Each line has either one mistake or no mistake. For each line, work out which group of words contains a mistake and mark the letter on your answer sheet. Mark N if there is no mistake.

Example

William expressed his sincere disapointment that the conference was postponed.
          A   B   C   D   N

Answer

C *'disapointment' should be 'disappointment'.*

Try the practice question below.

P2 The theatrical performance was more sucsessful than the critics had anticipated.
      A   B   C   D   N

Choose the word which completes each passage correctly. Each passage needs to make sense and be written in correct English. Pick one of the five options and mark the letter on your answer sheet.

Example

The explorers remembered to pack **there they're them their these** compass
                                          A   B   C   D   E

in case they got lost on the expedition.

Answer

D *'their' is correct because it shows that the compass belongs to the explorers.*

Try the practice question below.

Penelope put up posters in an attempt to encourage the other students to participate

P3 **in with on to by** the charity fundraiser.
     A   B   C   D   E

End of Practice Questions

Do not go on until you are told to

Read this passage carefully and answer the questions that follow.
You have **25 minutes** to complete this section, which contains 30 questions.

Strome Castle

Not much to see?

Strome Castle on the west coast of the Scottish Highlands may not be much to look at today. Sitting on a rocky piece of land which juts out into Loch Carron, only a few crumbled ruins remain. As you walk around these unassuming ruins, it may be difficult to imagine what the castle would have looked like in its prime. However, Strome Castle has a fascinating and turbulent past and is positioned in a spectacular location.

Trouble brewing

Strome Castle was built in the 1400s — it consisted of a square tower to the east and a courtyard to the west, the land on three of its sides dropping down abruptly towards large jagged rocks and the sea below. Loch Carron used to be a very busy waterway and the castle's location enabled it to keep a watchful eye on the vessels that went past. Thanks to its elevated position, the castle must have looked very impressive.

Like many castles, it wasn't to have a peaceful existence. It became the object of a dispute between two Scottish clans, the Macdonalds and the Mackenzies. It stood on the border of lands claimed by the two clans and over the years they competed for control of it. In 1539, King James V of Scotland gave Strome Castle to a branch of the Macdonald clan, but this didn't end the conflict over the castle. In around 1602, the Mackenzies surrounded the castle, trapping the Macdonalds inside.

Legend has it...

It is said that during this attack two Macdonald women drew water from the well inside the castle. However, they were nervous under the circumstances and in the dim light they poured the water into the barrel containing gunpowder instead of the water barrel. When the Macdonald men found out, they berated the women for what they had done.

Unfortunately, a prisoner inside the castle who was from the Mackenzie clan heard the commotion. He managed to escape and told the Mackenzie chief what had happened with the gunpowder. The Macdonalds surrendered and the Mackenzies allowed them to leave the castle with their belongings. The Mackenzie chief decided to blow up the castle and it is this explosion which helps explain why so very little of the castle remains.

In ruins

The castle's tower seemingly bore the brunt of the explosion, as none of it is left standing today. The remains of it can be seen in piles of rubble and stone, some of which lie an impressive distance from where the tower used to stand. Sizeable sections of the courtyard walls still remain, however. These ruins may suggest how thick the walls were and in one of them there is a large archway, facing the sea. The only sign of modern interference are railings which have been put in place between the gaps in the walls.

Answer these questions about the text. You can refer back to the text if you need to.
Pick the best answer and mark its letter on your answer sheet.

1 Why does the author think the castle "may not be much to look at" (lines 3-4)?

A The view from the castle isn't very nice.
B The author doesn't approve of the castle's design.
C Not much of the castle has survived.
D The castle wasn't very well constructed.
E The castle is surrounded by busy waterways.

2 Where is the castle located?

A On an island in Loch Carron
B To the west of Loch Carron
C At the bottom of a hill on the shore of Loch Carron
D Opposite the place where Loch Carron meets the sea
E On a rocky outcrop overlooking Loch Carron

3 According to the passage, what is the most appealing aspect of the castle?

A The fact that not a lot of the castle remains
B The beautiful surroundings it was built in
C Trying to imagine what it was like living in the castle
D Walking around the ruins
E The medieval architecture

4 According to the passage, why was the castle built where it was?

A For strategic reasons
B Because there weren't many houses there
C Because the ground there was stable
D So that boats could easily see the castle as they went by
E So that the Macdonalds had a good view of Skye

5 According to the passage, which of these statements is true?

A The Macdonalds and Mackenzies claimed neighbouring lands.
B The Macdonalds and Mackenzies used to share the castle.
C King James V gave the castle to the Mackenzies.
D The Macdonalds tried to take the castle from the Mackenzies.
E The Mackenzies rebelled against the rule of King James V.

6 What did the Mackenzies do in around 1602?

A They asked King James V to give them the castle.
B They declared war on the Macdonalds.
C They came to the castle to negotiate with the Macdonalds.
D They attacked King James V.
E They tried to make the Macdonalds surrender the castle.

Turn over to the next page

7 Why do you think the women were nervous?

  A They weren't sure where to pour the water after they drew it from the well.
  B They were fearful because their castle was under attack.
  C They were scared of getting in trouble.
  D They couldn't see where they were going.
  E They were worried they would drop the water.

8 Why did the Macdonalds surrender?

  A They could no longer defend themselves.
  B They were running out of food and water.
  C Their prisoner had escaped.
  D The Mackenzies offered them land if they surrendered.
  E The Mackenzies threatened to blow up the castle.

9 The text suggests that the railings:

  A are unnecessary.
  B were put up without permission.
  C have become rusty over time.
  D spoil the enjoyment of walking around the ruins.
  E have been added relatively recently.

Answer these questions about the meaning of words as they are used in the text.

10 Which of these words is closest in meaning to "unassuming" (line 7)?

  A Peaceful
  B Dull
  C Modest
  D Dramatic
  E Decaying

11 Which of these words is closest in meaning to "abruptly" (line 18)?

  A Shortly
  B Steeply
  C Roughly
  D Harshly
  E Hurriedly

12 Which of the following words is closest in meaning to "berated" (line 46)?

  A Applauded
  B Scolded
  C Punished
  D Humiliated
  E Shouted

Answer these questions about the way words and phrases are used in the text.

13 The word "turbulent" (line 11) is an example of which part of speech?

- A Verb
- B Noun
- C Article
- D Adjective
- E Adverb

14 "It is said that during this attack two Macdonald women drew water from the well inside the castle" (lines 39-41). What is the subject of this sentence?

- A this attack
- B two Macdonald women
- C water
- D the well
- E the castle

15 The text says that the tower "bore the brunt of the explosion" (lines 61-62).
What is meant by this?

- A The tower wasn't affected by the explosion.
- B The tower was the only thing to explode.
- C The explosion was set off in the tower.
- D The tower suffered the most in the explosion.
- E People hid in the tower during the explosion.

Turn over to the next page

This passage contains some spelling mistakes. Each numbered line has either one mistake or no mistake. For each line, work out which group of words contains a mistake, and mark the letter on your answer sheet. Mark N if there is no mistake.

Solar Eclipses

16. A solar eclipse ocurs when the moon moves between the Earth and the sun, sometimes

17. obscureing the sun from view. Total eclipses are extremely rare to observe. This is

18. because they require the Earth, sun and moon to be in perfect allignment. However,

19. partial eclipses, where only a fractian of the sun is blocked, are much more frequent.

20. It's important to wear protective glasses when witnessing this spectacular event.

This passage contains some mistakes involving capital letters and punctuation. Each numbered line has either one mistake or no mistake. For each line, work out which group of words contains a mistake and mark the letter on your answer sheet. Mark N if there is no mistake.

Alice's Bad Mood

21. "Why do we have to go?" moaned Alice, slamming the door, of the car.
    A — B — C — D — N

22. "You have to go to the dentist", replied Alice's mother sternly. "It's important."
    A — B — C — D — N

23. As the car pulled out of the driveway Alice sulked in the back. She was furious with
    A — B — C — D — N

24. her mum for booking the appointment at this time: it meant she had to miss the
    A — B — C — D — N

25. latest episode of 'Detective Daisy'. She didnt think the day could get any worse.
    A — B — C — D — N

Turn over to the next page

For each numbered line, choose the word, or group of words, which completes the passage correctly. The passage needs to make sense and be written in correct English. Pick one of the five options and mark the letter on your answer sheet.

The Interview

26 The doors were already closing as Ahmed slipped **on to / into / onto / in to / out** the train.
　　　　　　　　　　　　　　　　　　　　　　　　　　　　A　　　B　　　C　　　D　　　E

27 As he **caught / had caught / catching / catched / catch** his breath, Ahmed noticed his
　　　　　A　　　　　B　　　　　C　　　　　D　　　　E

reflection in the window. He looked unkempt — not like he was about to interview to be a

28 secret agent. He **would of / would have / wouldn't / would / could** ironed his shirt, but the
　　　　　　　　　　　A　　　　　B　　　　　C　　　　D　　　E

29 call had been **very / so / this / really / slightly** unexpected that he'd rushed out of the door.
　　　　　　　　　A　　B　　C　　　D　　　E

30 He'd barely had time to grab his coat **after / upon / without / before / during** setting off to
　　　　　　　　　　　　　　　　　　　　　A　　　B　　　C　　　D　　　E

complete his first challenge — finding the secret base.

End of Section 1

Do not go on until you are told to

Section 2: Verbal Reasoning

Example and Practice Questions

You have **5 minutes** to complete practice questions P1 to P5. Read the examples carefully and mark your answers to the practice questions on the answer sheet.

Find the pair of letters that continues each sequence in the best way.
Use the alphabet to help you.

A B C D E F G H I J K L M N O P Q R S T U V W X Y Z

Example   AZ   AY   BX   BW   (?)

    A CV   **B** DV   **C** CW   **D** DT   **E** DW

Answer   **CV**   *The first letter in each pair repeats once, then moves forward 1 letter. The second letter moves back 1 letter each time.*

Try the practice question below.

P1   DW   HV   LU   PT   (?)

    A TX   **B** RS   **C** TS   **D** WR   **E** RT

Three of the words in each list are linked. Find the two words that are **not** related to these three and mark them **both** on the answer sheet.

Example   cup   plate   table   dish   drink

    A cup   **B** plate   **C** table   **D** dish   **E** drink

Answer   **table** and **drink**   *The other three are containers that you can eat or drink from.*

Try the practice question below.

P2   actor   director   dancer   singer   spectator

    A actor   **B** director   **C** dancer   **D** singer   **E** spectator

Turn over to the next page

Find the three-letter word that completes the word in capital letters, and so finishes the sentence in a sensible way.

Example   The king wore his golden **CN**.

    A APE   **B** ROT   **C** ROW   **D** RAW   **E** LAW

Answer   **ROW**   *The complete word is* **CROWN**.

Try the practice question below.

P3 Brian tried to stop the boat from **SING** below the waves.

    A INK   **B** LAY   **C** NOW   **D** EAT   **E** HOW

Find the number that continues each sequence in the best way.

Example   4, 8, 12, 16, (?)

    A 16   **B** 18   **C** 20   **D** 24   **E** 26

Answer   **20**   *Add 4 each time.*

Try the practice question below.

P4 19, 16, 13, 10, (?)

    A 1   **B** 4   **C** 7   **D** 8   **E** 9

Find two words, one from each set of brackets, that go together to form a new word. Mark **both** words on the answer sheet.

Example   (letter copy word) (hole box sure)

    A letter   **X** hole
    B copy   **Y** box
    C word   **Z** sure

Answer   **letter** and **box**   *'letterbox' is the only correctly spelled word that can be made.*

Try the practice question below.

P5 (stage enter glare)   (trance ring prise)

    A stage   **X** trance
    B enter   **Y** ring
    C glare   **Z** prise

End of Practice Questions
Do not go on until you are told to

You have **20 minutes** to complete this section, which contains 25 questions.

Find the pair of letters that continues each sequence in the best way.
Use the alphabet to help you.

A B C D E F G H I J K L M N O P Q R S T U V W X Y Z

Example	AZ AY BX BW (?)				
	A CV	**B** DV	**C** CW	**D** DT	**E** DW
Answer	CV				

1 TC RF PI NL (?)
   A LH   **B** NP   **C** NH   **D** LO   **E** JH

2 FK HM GO IQ HS (?)
   A IT   **B** JV   **C** JU   **D** KW   **E** FT

3 EA EB DD DG CK (?)
   A CQ   **B** DN   **C** BO   **D** CP   **E** BP

4 XB VD UE SG RH (?)
   A TK   **B** TI   **C** PI   **D** OJ   **E** PJ

5 TV QT RR OP PN (?)
   A ML   **B** NO   **C** MJ   **D** NL   **E** QI

Turn over to the next page

Three of the words in each list are linked. Find the two words that are **not** related to these three and mark them **both** on the answer sheet.

Example	cup plate table dish drink
	A cup **B** plate **C** table **D** dish **E** drink
Answer	**table** and **drink**

6 emperor   king   minister   sultan   knight
   A emperor   **B** king   **C** minister   **D** sultan   **E** knight

7 oversee   analyse   manage   supervise   scrutinise
   A oversee   **B** analyse   **C** manage   **D** supervise   **E** scrutinise

8 competent   ingenious   inventive   haughty   resourceful
   A competent   **B** ingenious   **C** inventive   **D** haughty   **E** resourceful

9 road   trail   journey   pathway   trip
   A road   **B** trail   **C** journey   **D** pathway   **E** trip

10 acorn   twig   willow   chestnut   birch
   A acorn   **B** twig   **C** willow   **D** chestnut   **E** birch

---

Find the three-letter word that completes the word in capital letters, and so finishes the sentence in a sensible way.

Example	The king wore his golden **CN**.
	A APE **B** ROT **C** ROW **D** RAW **E** LAW
Answer	**ROW** (the complete word is **CROWN**)

11 Sunita felt **REVED** that it was the summer holidays.
   A PRO   **B** AMP   **C** CUR   **D** LIE   **E** ALE

12 Oscar **SCED** his knee against the concrete.
   A OWL   **B** RIB   **C** RAP   **D** OFF   **E** OLD

13 Five **CES** of apples were stacked in the cellar.
    A HID   B RAN   C HIM   D RIM   E RAT

14 The **SCH** continues for the lost dog.
    A EAR   B TAR   C WIT   D COT   E TEN

15 The teacher spent his evening **MING** the homework.
    A ILK   B ARK   C ASK   D END   E AIM

Find the number that continues each sequence in the best way.

Example   4, 8, 12, 16, (?)
    A 16   B 18   C 20   D 24   E 26

Answer   20

16 36, 32, 28, 24, (?)
    A 16   B 18   C 20   D 22   E 26

17 3, 6, 12, 24, (?)
    A 30   B 34   C 36   D 40   E 48

18 4, 6, 10, 16, 24, (?)
    A 28   B 30   C 32   D 34   E 36

19 2, 34, 50, 58, 62, (?)
    A 64   B 66   C 68   D 70   E 74

20 50, 45, 38, 29, 18, (?)
    A 3   B 5   C 11   D 15   E 17

Turn over to the next page

Find **two** words, one from each set of brackets, that go together to form a new word.
Mark **both** words on the answer sheet.

Example   (letter copy word)   (hole box sure)

A letter
B copy
C word

X hole
Y box
Z sure

Answer   letter and box = letterbox

21 (up over fur)   (owe lode roar)
A up
B over
C fur

X owe
Y lode
Z roar

22 (for after too)   (thought night live)
A for
B after
C too

X thought
Y night
Z live

23 (bed bead heed)   (stone rock rag)
A bed
B bead
C heed

X stone
Y rock
Z rag

24 (plot pollute accept)   (ants age able)
A plot
B pollute
C accept

X ants
Y age
Z able

25 (heir handle heel)   (brush loom tear)
A heir
B handle
C heel

X brush
Y loom
Z tear

End of test

CGP

11+ Practice Paper

Set A: Paper 2
Mathematical & Non-Verbal Skills

For the GL Buckinghamshire Transfer Test

Read the following:

Do not open this booklet or start the test until you are told to do so.

1. This is a multiple-choice test. You will have around one hour to complete this paper, including the practice questions and reading time.

2. There are 2 sections in this test — Non-Verbal & Spatial Reasoning and Maths.

3. Section 1 — Non-Verbal & Spatial Reasoning is divided into smaller subsections. Each subsection starts with some examples showing you how to answer the questions. You will be given time at the start of each subsection to complete the practice questions. You will then have 5 minutes to complete each subsection.

4. You will have 5 minutes to complete the practice questions at the start of Section 2 — Maths. You will then have 25 minutes to complete the second section, which contains 23 questions.

5. You should mark your answer to each question in pencil on the separate answer sheet.

6. You should only mark one answer for each question. To mark your answer, draw a straight line through the rectangle next to the option you have chosen. If you make a mistake, rub it out and mark your new answer clearly.

7. Make sure you keep your place on the answer sheet and mark your answer in the box that has the same number as the question.

8. Do as many questions as you can. If you get stuck on a question, choose the answer that you think is most likely to be correct, then move on to the next question.

9. You should do any rough working on a separate piece of paper.

Work carefully, but go as quickly as you can.

Section 1: Non-Verbal & Spatial Reasoning

Example and Practice Questions

Each question below has five figures. Find which figure in each row is **most unlike** the others. **Mark its letter** on the **answer sheet**.

Example

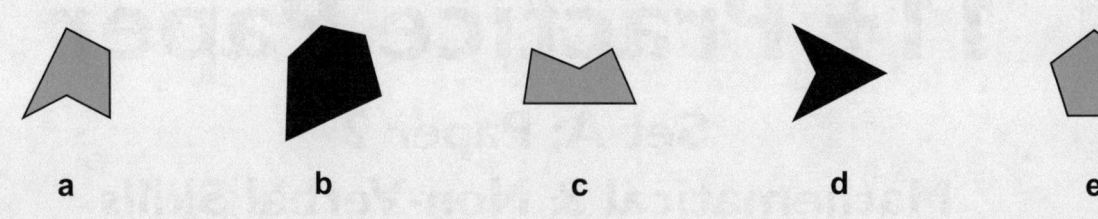

Answer: d *In all other figures, the shape has five sides.*

Try these two practice questions below:

P1

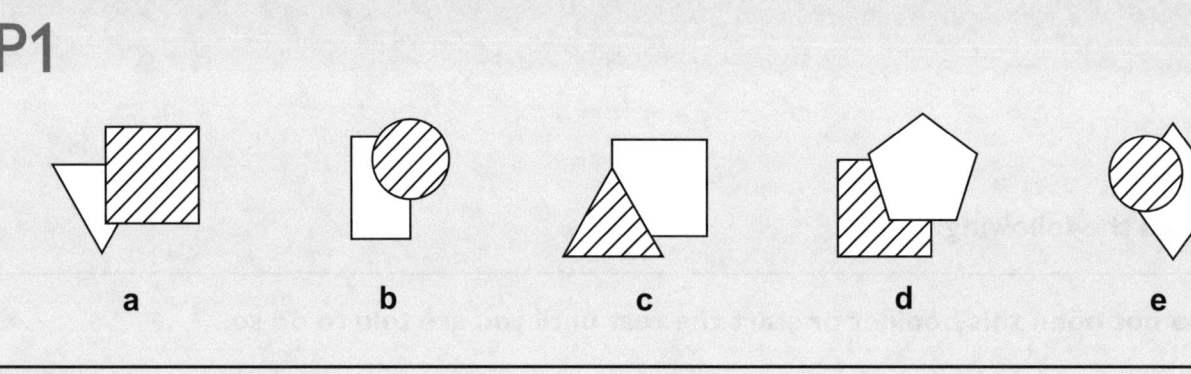

P2

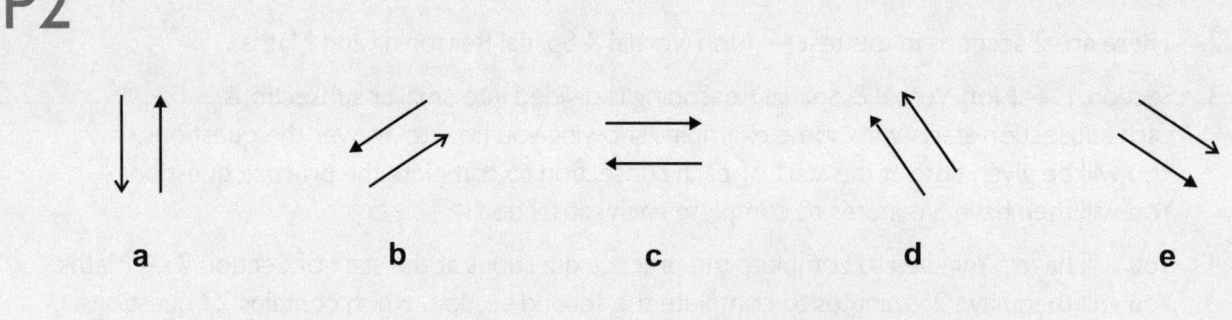

End of Practice Questions. Do not go on until you are told to.

You have **5 minutes** to complete this subsection, which contains 7 questions.

1

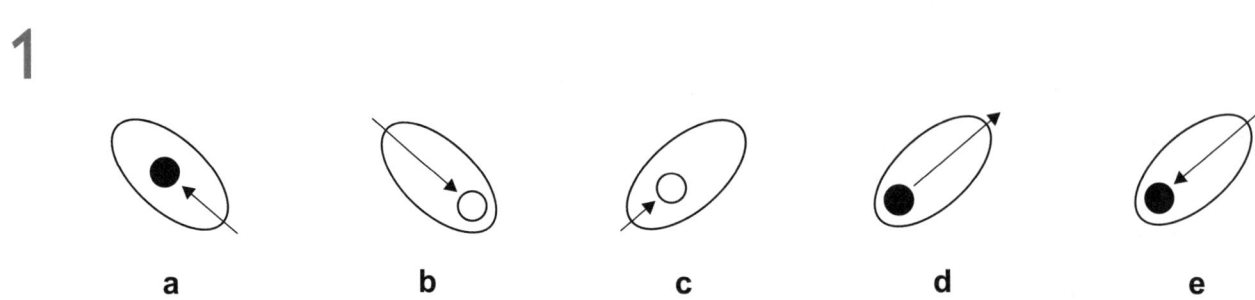

Now go to the next question

2

a b c d e

3

a b c d e

4

a b c d e

5

a b c d e

6

a b c d e

7

a b c d e

Do not go on until you are told to

 © CGP 2019

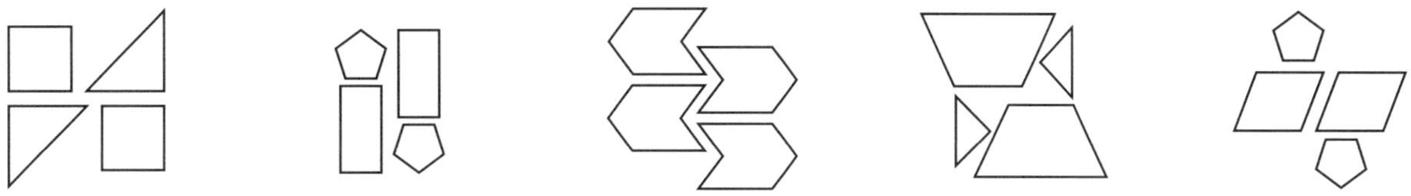

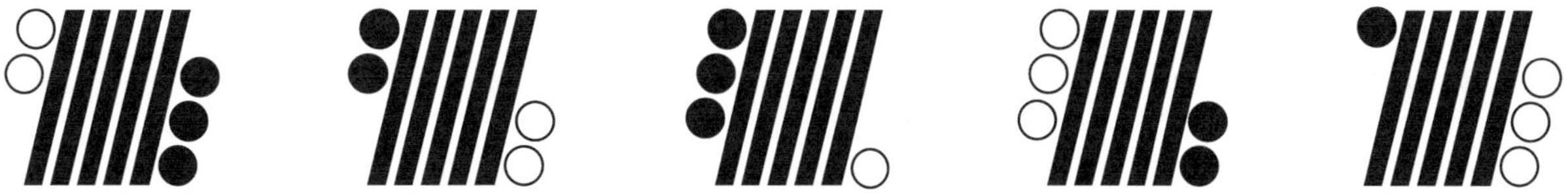

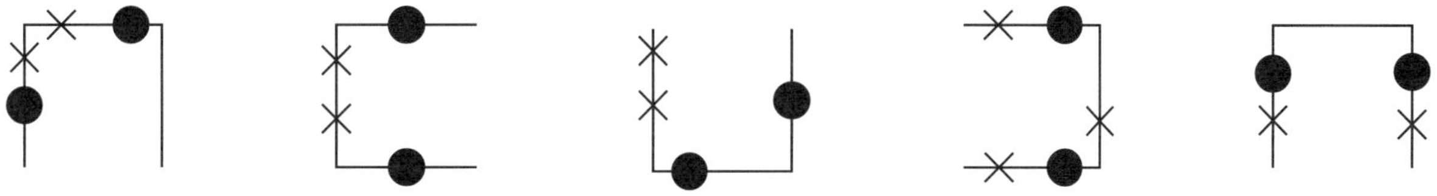

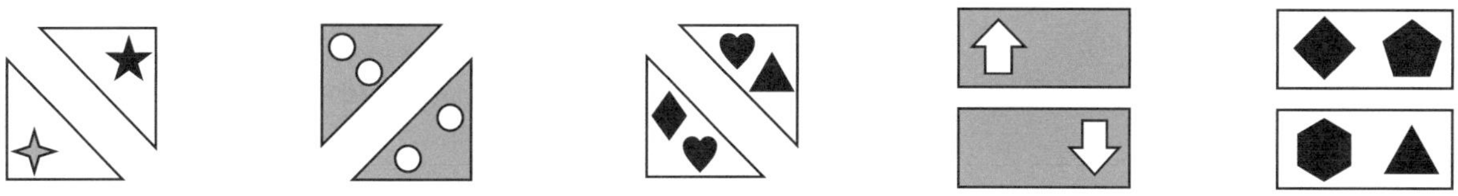

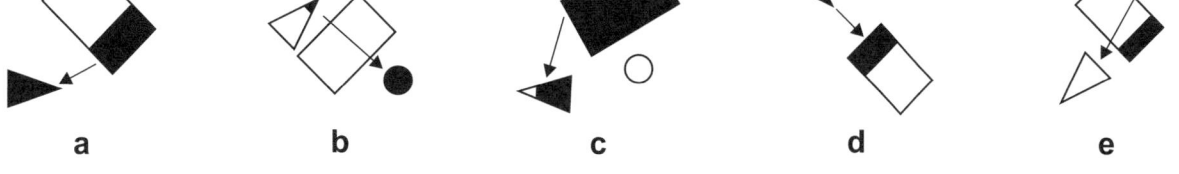

Example and Practice Questions

On the left of each question below is a big square with one small empty square. Find which of the five squares on the right should replace the empty square. **Mark its letter** on the **answer sheet**.

Example

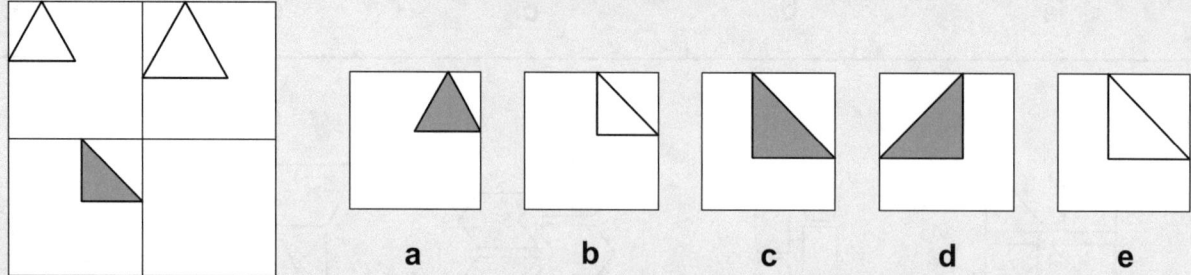

Answer: c *Working from left to right, the shape increases in size.*

Try these two practice questions below:

1

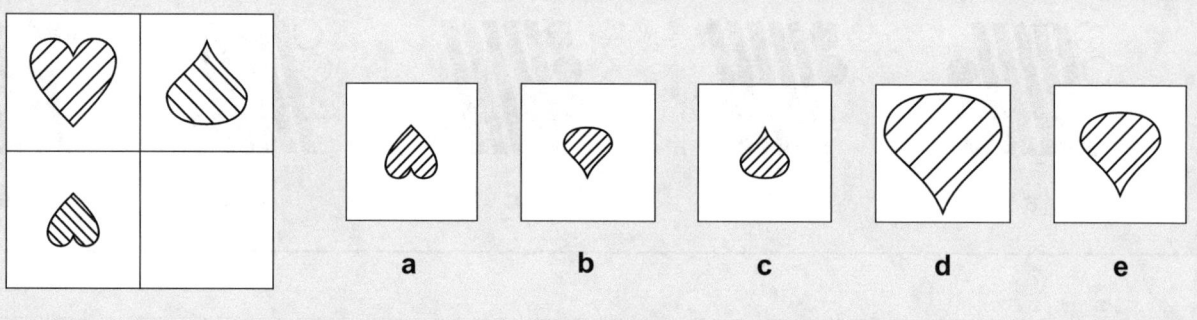

P2

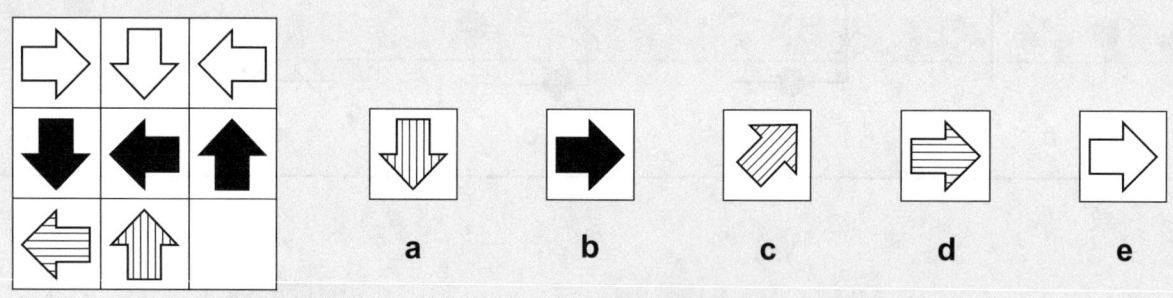

End of Practice Questions. Do not go on until you are told to.

You have **5 minutes** to complete this subsection, which contains 7 questions.

8

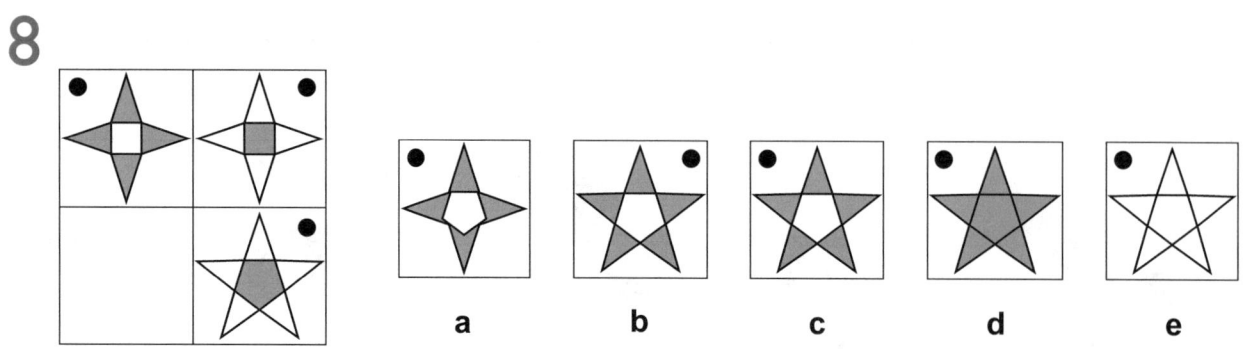

Now go to the next question

9

a b c d e

10

a b c d e

11

a b c d e

12

a b c d e

13

a b c d e

14

a b c d e

Do not go on until you are told to

© CGP 2019

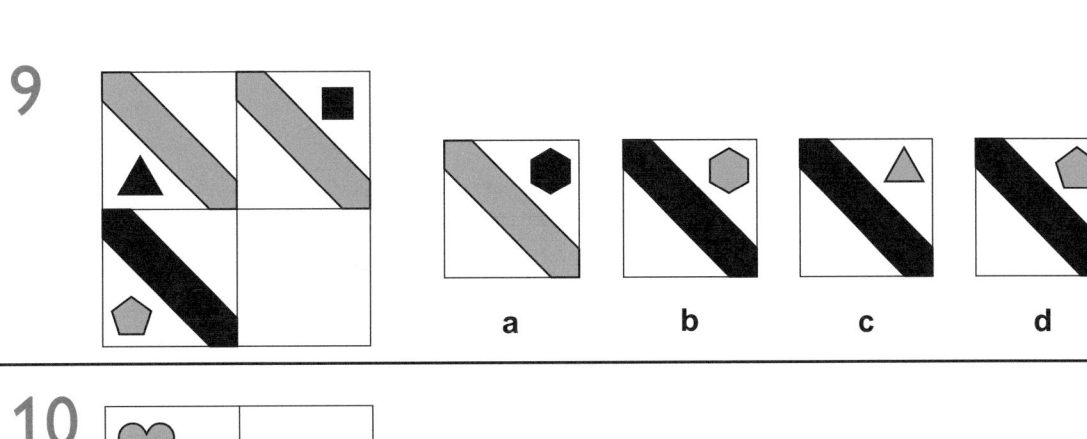

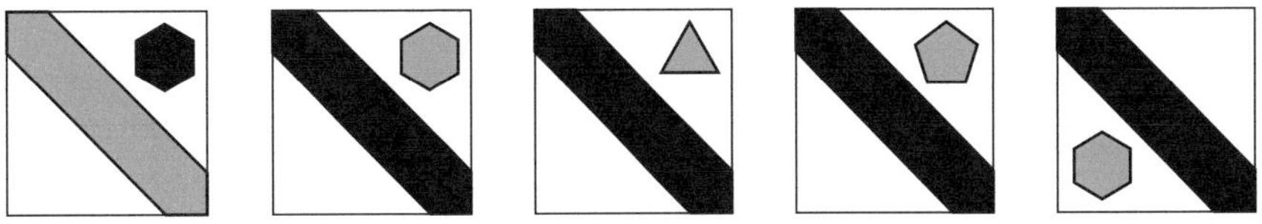

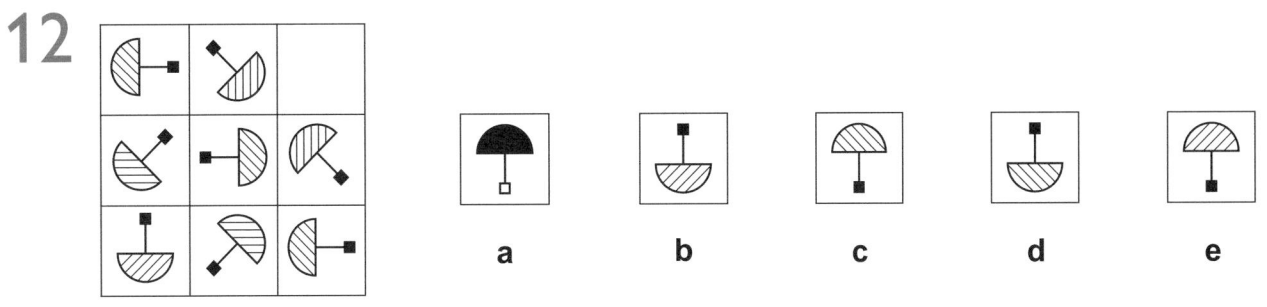

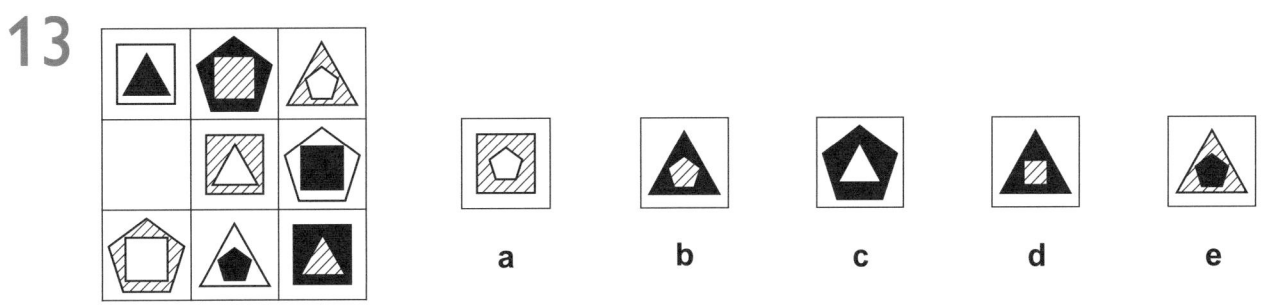

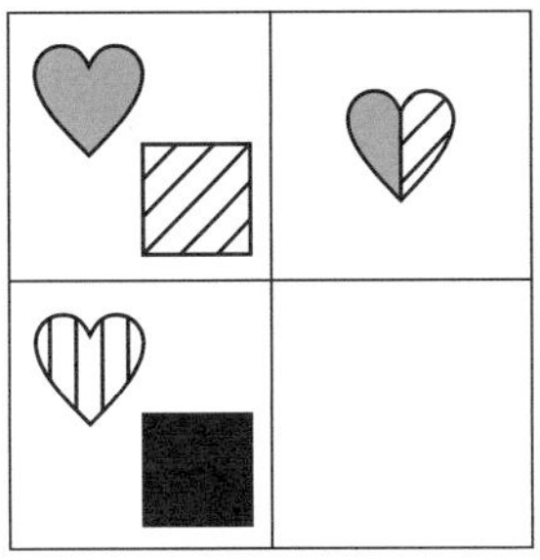

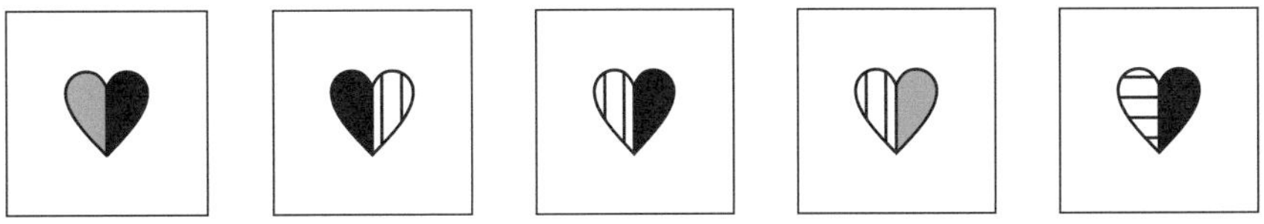

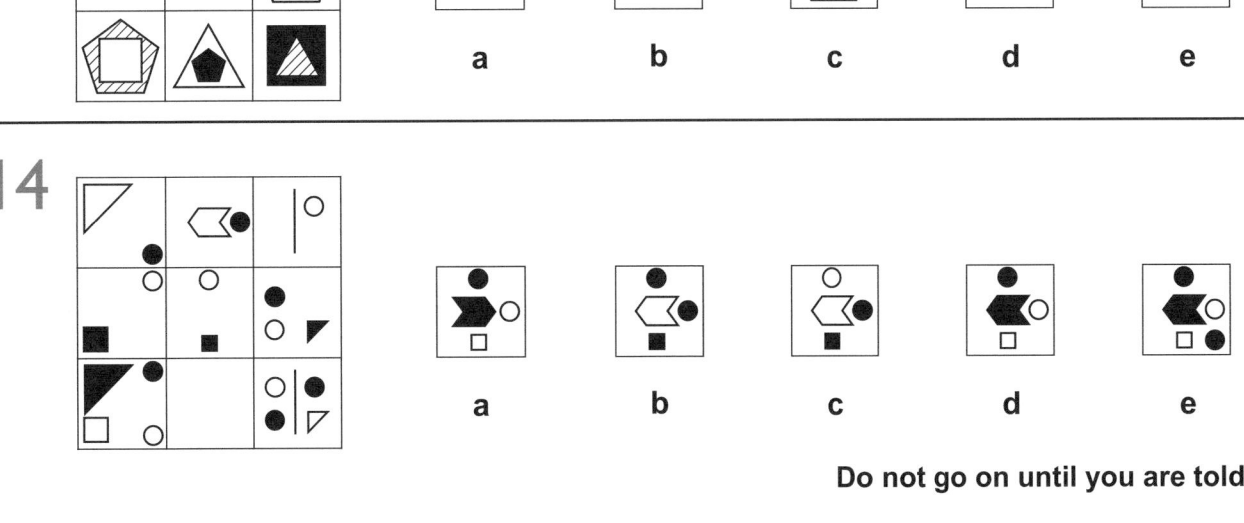

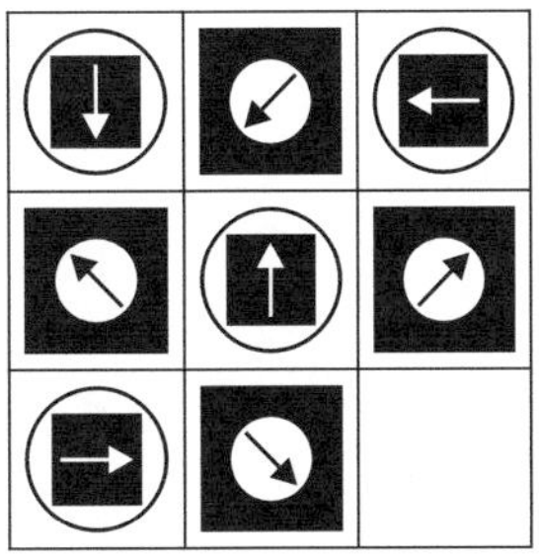

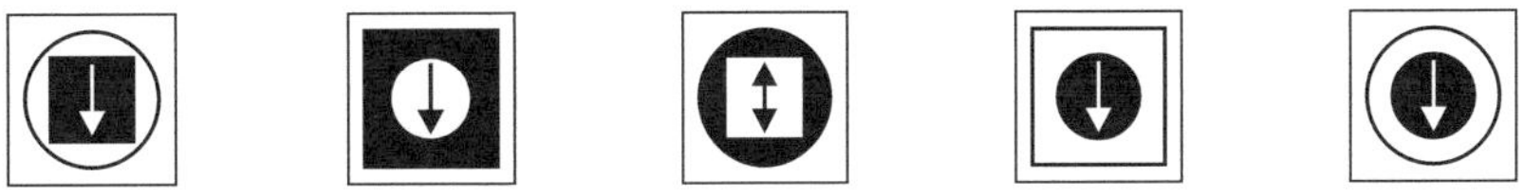

Example and Practice Questions

Work out which option contains the hidden shape shown. The hidden shape will always be the same size, but it might have been rotated. **Mark its letter** on the **answer sheet**.

Example

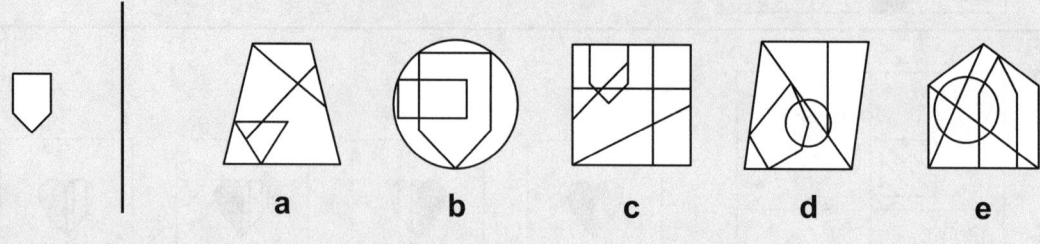

Answer: c

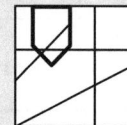

Try these two practice questions below:

P1

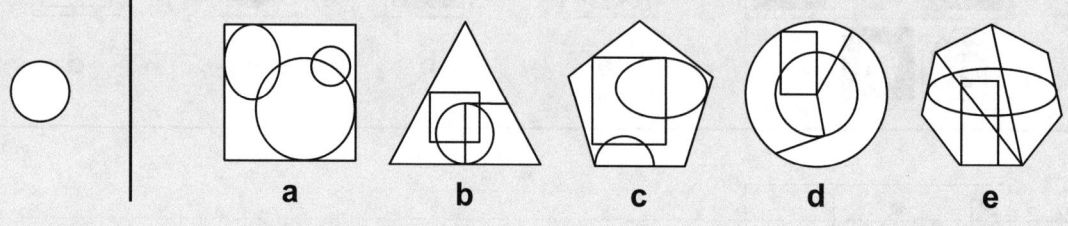

P2

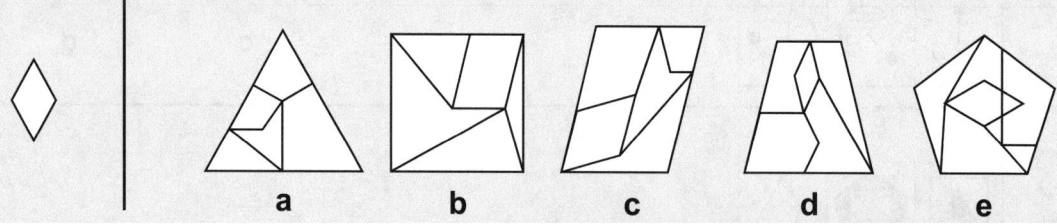

End of Practice Questions. Do not go on until you are told to.

You have **5 minutes** to complete this subsection, which contains 7 questions.

15

Now go to the next question

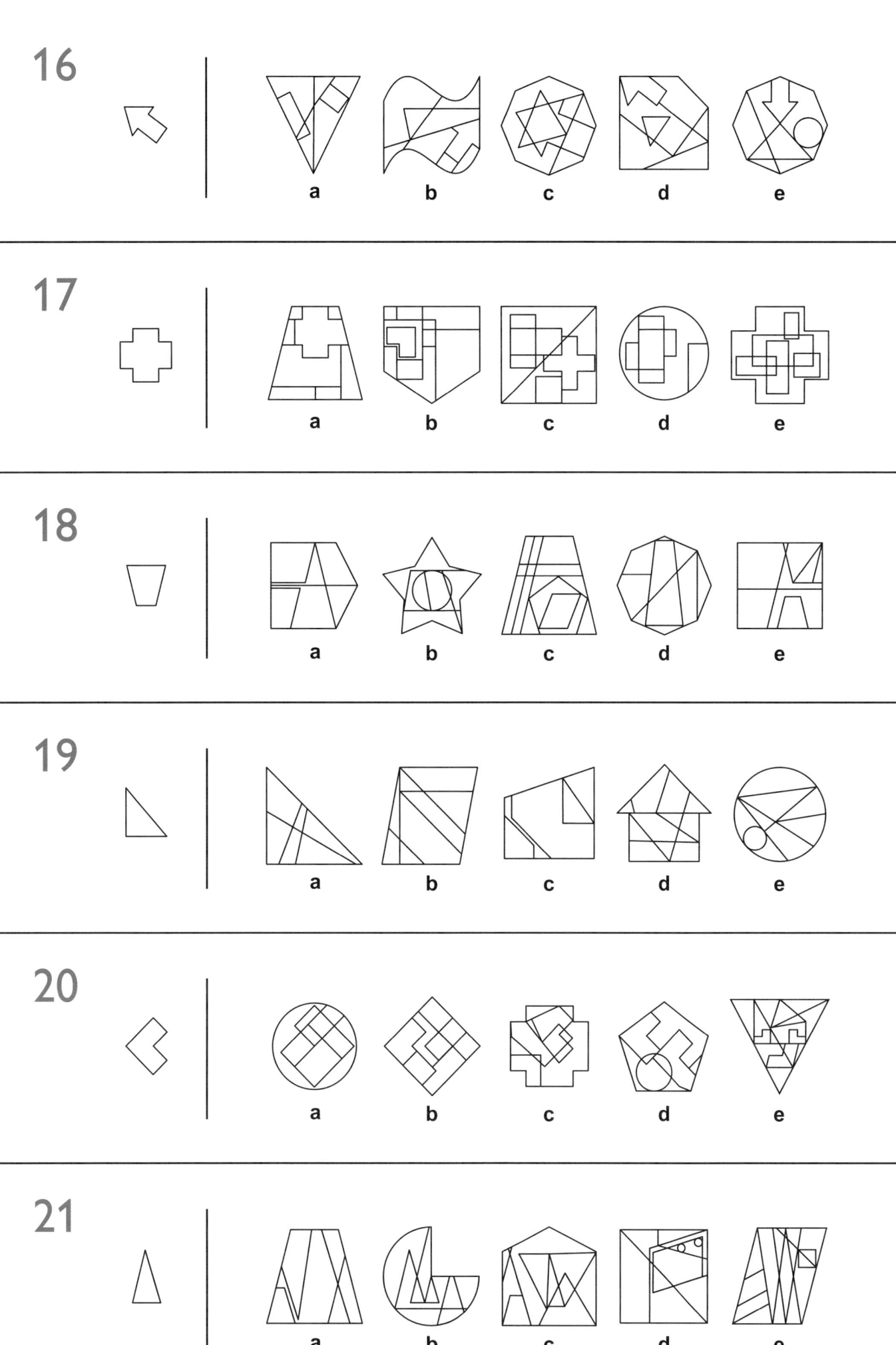

Example and Practice Questions

Work out which option is a top-down 2D view of the 3D figure on the left.
Mark its letter on the **answer sheet**.

Example

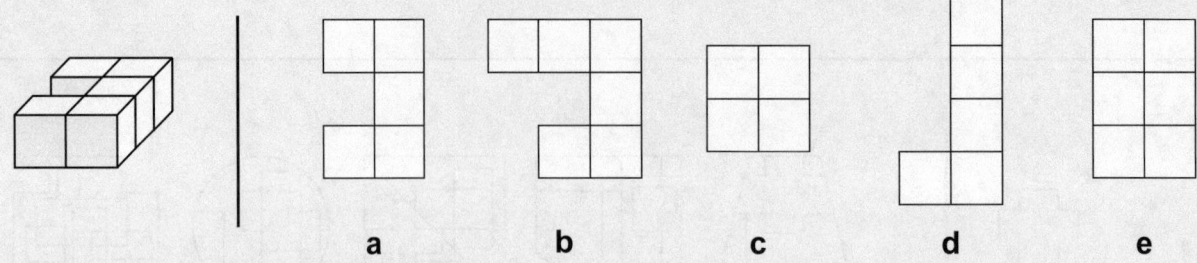

Answer: a *There are five blocks visible from above, which rules out options b, c and e.*
There are two blocks visible at the back, which rules out option d.

Try these two practice questions below:

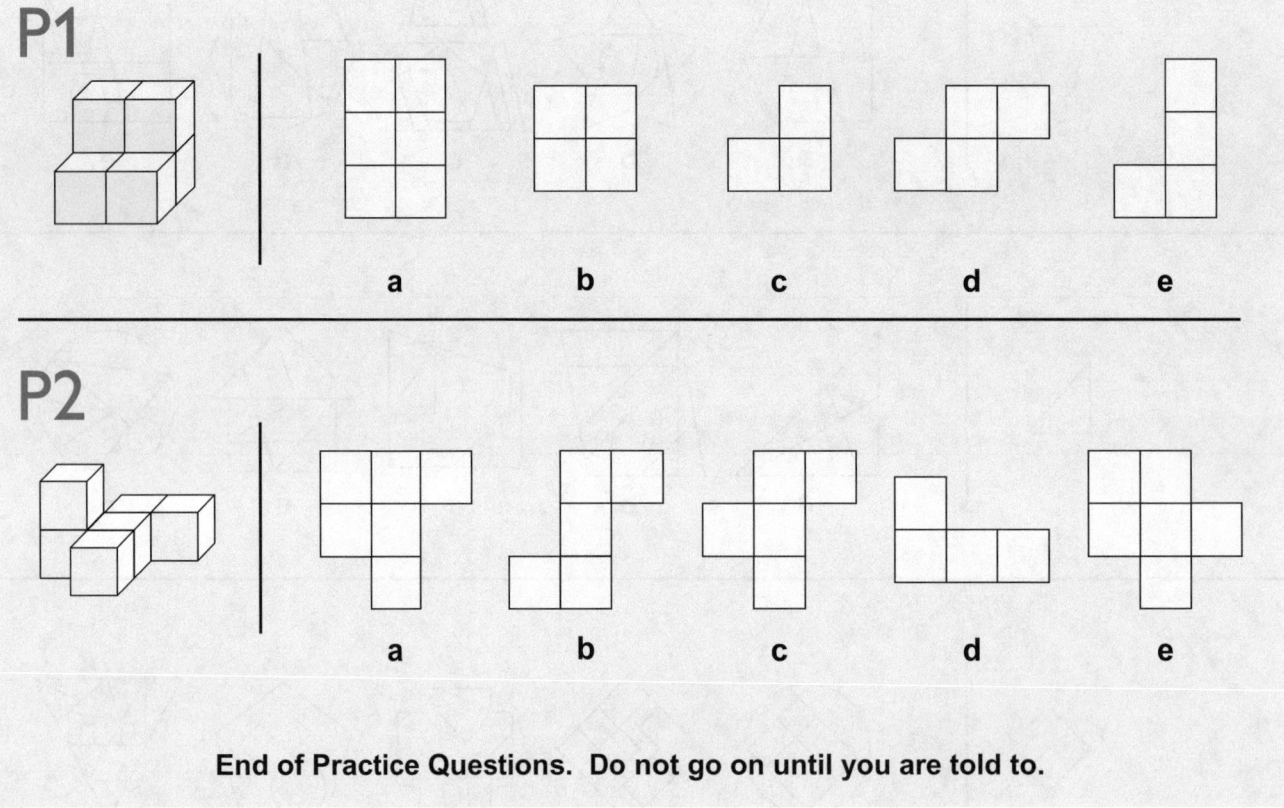

End of Practice Questions. Do not go on until you are told to.

You have **5 minutes** to complete this subsection, which contains 7 questions.

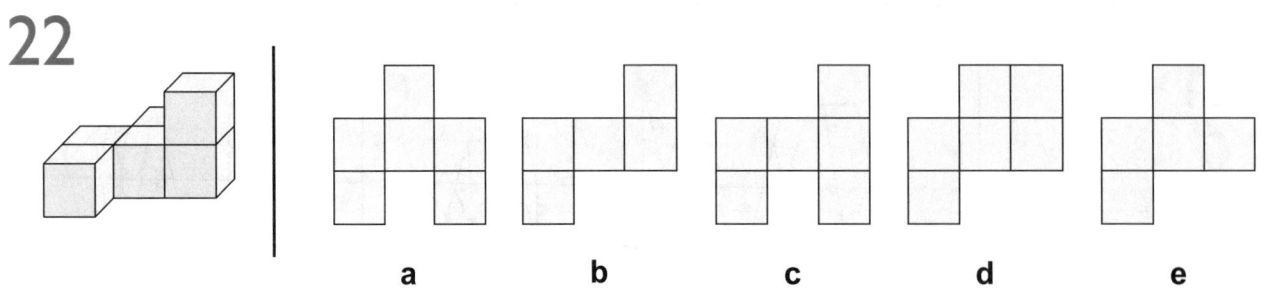

Now go to the next question

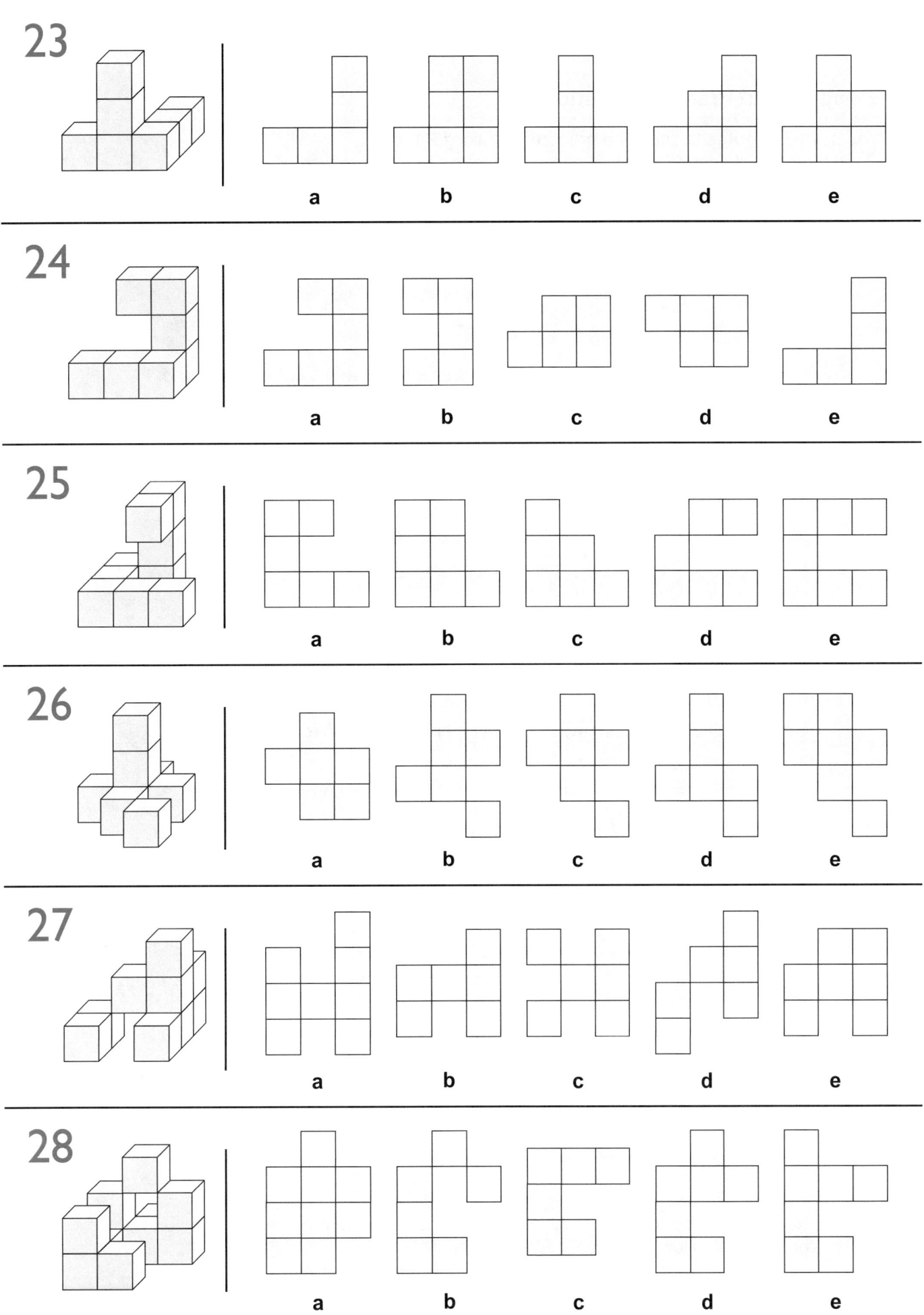

End of Section 1

Do not go on until you are told to

Section 2: Maths

Example and Practice Questions

You have **5 minutes** to complete practice questions P1 to P3.
Read the example carefully before attempting to answer the practice questions.

Example

Which of the following fractions is equivalent to $^6/_8$?

A $^3/_4$ B $^1/_2$ C $^{10}/_{16}$ D $^{18}/_{36}$ E $^1/_5$

Answer

$^3/_4$ The numerator and denominator in the fraction $^6/_8$ have a common factor of 2.
This means that you can simplify $^6/_8$ by dividing the top and the bottom by 2.

$$^6/_8 = {^{6 \div 2}}/_{8 \div 2} = {^3}/_4$$

Try the practice questions below:

P1 Nassima bought 6 footballs. Each football cost £2.99.
How much did she spend in total?

A £17.94   B £18.00   C £6.00   D £19.74   E £18.64

P2 George draws a graph showing a flight by his remote-control model plane.

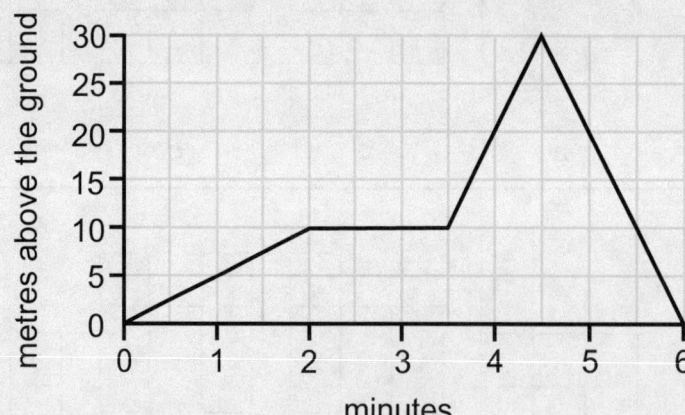

How high was the plane after 4 minutes of flight?

A 30 m   B 20 m   C 10 m   D 0 m   E 5 m

P3 Nadiya has a sack of soil weighing 15 kg. She fills plant pots with 3400 g of soil each. How many plant pots can she fill?

A 14   B 2   C 8   D 4   E 6

End of Practice Questions

Do not go on until you are told to

The following questions will test your mathematical skills.
You will have **25 minutes** to complete this section, which contains 23 questions.

1 Maria drives to work every weekday. This week, her car used 45.972 litres of petrol. What is this volume rounded to the nearest ten litres?

  A 50 litres   B 45 litres   C 40 litres   D 46 litres   E 60 litres

2 What is 15% of 140?

  A 14   B 70   C 20   D 27   E 21

3 Leo wants to cycle 150 miles across four training sessions this week.
So far he has cycled 21 miles, 52 miles and 34 miles.
How far does he need to cycle in his final training session?

  A 53 miles   B 47 miles   C 23 miles   D 43 miles   E 97 miles

4 7245 × 83 = 601 335. What is 7.245 × 8.3?

  A 6013.35   B 60.1335   C 6.01335   D 601.335   E 0.601335

5 Pupils in a class recorded what transport they use to get to school.
They put the information in this bar graph.

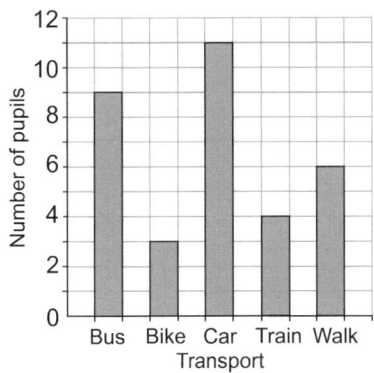

How many more pupils travel by car than by bike?

  A 11   B 2   C 7   D 8   E 6

6 Which estimate best describes the length of a double-decker bus?

  A 11 m   B 11 cm   C 1.1 km   D 1100 mm   E 1.1 m

Turn over to the next page

7 What is the volume of this cuboid?

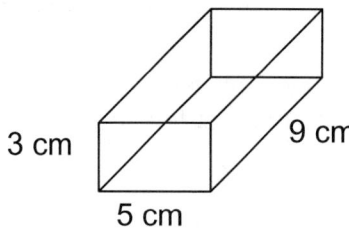

- **A** 76 cm³
- **B** 180 cm³
- **C** 48 cm³
- **D** 17 cm³
- **E** 135 cm³

8 The grid below shows where Joss' house is. He wants to climb to the summit of a mountain which is 4 squares west of his house. What are the coordinates of the summit?

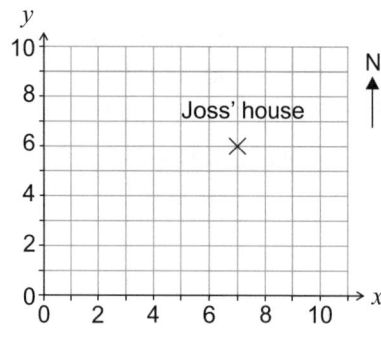

- **A** (6, 11)
- **B** (4, 6)
- **C** (11, 6)
- **D** (3, 6)
- **E** (7, 4)

9 Anna has set up a lemonade stall outside her house. 2 lemons make 3.5 glasses of lemonade. In one morning, Anna sells 42 glasses of lemonade. How many lemons did she use?

- **A** 22
- **B** 24
- **C** 26
- **D** 28
- **E** 32

10 Phoebe recorded the types of dog she saw in the park one morning. The pie chart shows her data.

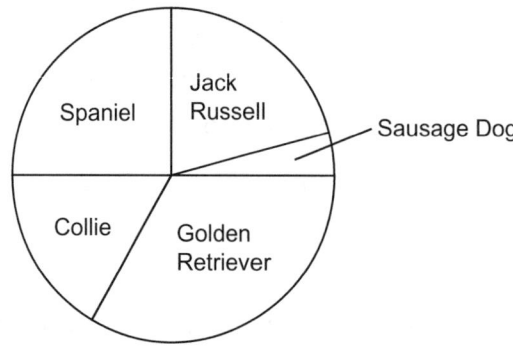

She saw twice as many Golden Retrievers as Collies.
If she saw 8 Golden Retrievers, how many dogs did she see in total?

- **A** 24
- **B** 12
- **C** 4
- **D** 16
- **E** 36

11 What is the size of the missing angle x in this right-angled triangle?

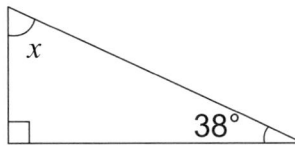

A 42° B 38° C 58° D 90° E 52°

12 In the equation $7a - 2 = 19$, what is the value of a?

A 2 B 3 C 4 D 5 E 6

13 Poe is a postman. He records the number of letters and parcels he delivers each day. The graph below shows Poe's deliveries this week. Poe doesn't work on Sundays.

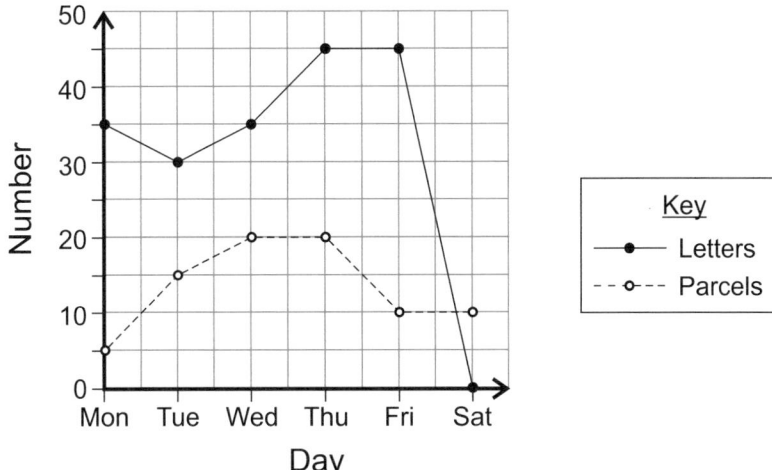

On what day did Poe deliver exactly half as many parcels as letters?

A Monday
B Tuesday
C Wednesday
D Thursday
E Friday

14 The diagram below shows the shape of a box.

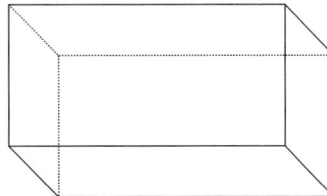

Which of the following best describes the shape of the box?

A Prism B Cube C Rectangle D Pyramid E Trapezium

15 A country has decided to introduce a new currency. The graph shown converts the country's old currency, Oldcoin, into its new currency, Newcoin.

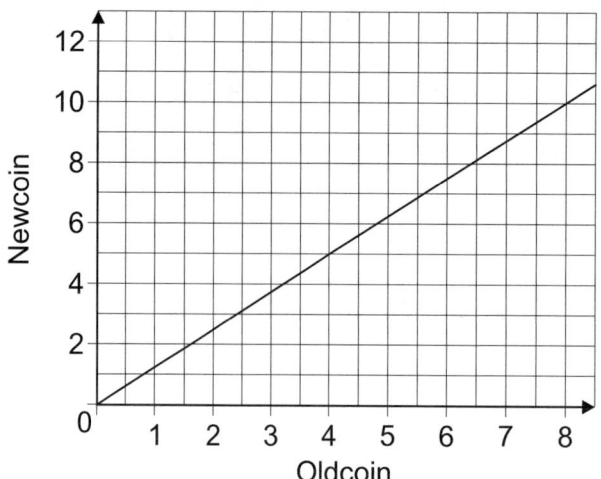

Claudia converts 4 Oldcoin. How many Newcoin does she receive?

A 6 **B** 4 **C** 3 **D** 7 **E** 5

16 Millom Community Park is made up of two rectangular grass fields, as shown in the diagram.

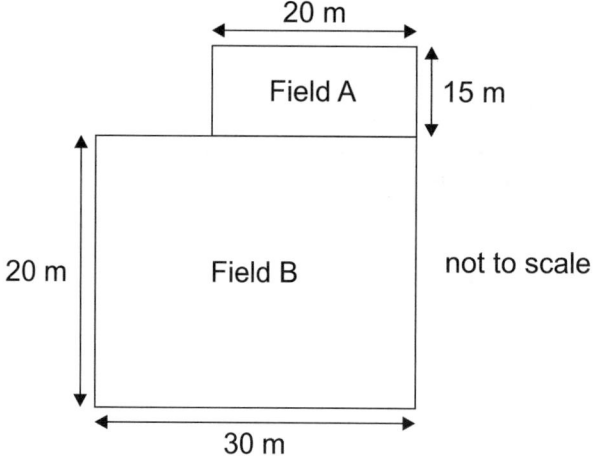

A fence goes right around the perimeter of Millom Community Park. What is the length of the fence?

A 900 m **B** 150 m **C** 130 m **D** 85 m **E** 100 m

17 Rafael records the number of his friends who complete an obstacle course each day. He has recorded last week's results in a table, shown below.

Day	Number of people
Monday	5
Tuesday	2
Wednesday	5
Thursday	1
Friday	7
Saturday	5
Sunday	3

What was the mean number of people to complete the obstacle course per day?

A 5   **B** 3   **C** 7   **D** 4   **E** 9

18 Felix draws a rhombus on a graph, shown below.

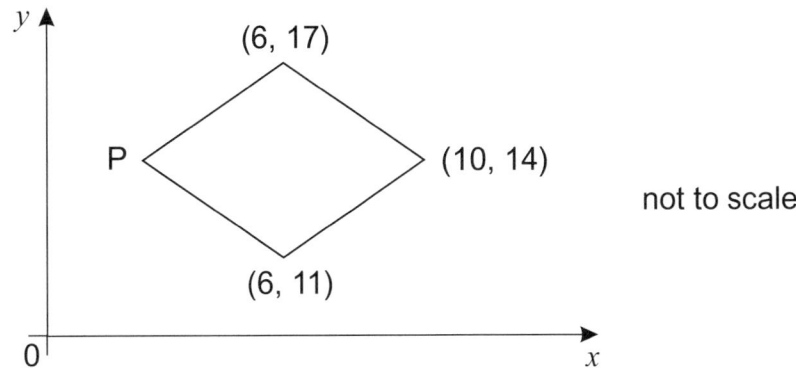

not to scale

What are the coordinates of point P?

A (10, 6)   **B** (4, 14)   **C** (2, 14)   **D** (14, 10)   **E** (2, 17)

19 Sonam, Lindsey and Robin are taking it in turns to play table tennis against each other. They play 30 matches in total and each match has one winner.
Lindsey wins 5 of the matches.

What fraction of the total number of matches did Lindsey win?

A $\frac{1}{6}$ **B** $\frac{5}{24}$ **C** $\frac{1}{2}$ **D** $\frac{5}{19}$ **E** $\frac{1}{4}$

20 Tilda owns a collection of teapots. She groups the teapots into three categories: Small, Medium and Large. She draws a pictogram of her collection.

Small	
Medium	
Large	

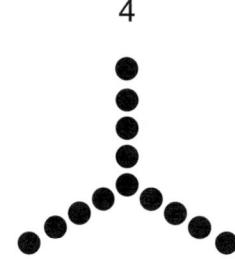 = 2 teapots

What proportion of Tilda's teapots are Large?

A 0.8   B 0.125   C 0.25   D 0.5   E 0.4

21 The shapes in the sequence below are made up of small pegs.

1   2   3   4

If n is the shape number, which of the following expressions describes the number of pegs in the shape?

A $3n + 3$ B $3n + 1$ C $n + 4$ D $4n + 3$ E $3n + 4$

22 A train from Birmingham to London normally departs at 13:30 and is scheduled to take two hours. Today the train set off 20 minutes late and had to stop for another 13 minutes when cows walked onto the line. At what time did the train arrive in London?

A 16:03   B 15:37   C 15:03   D 15:23   E 16:23

23 Santosh is making up an interesting number list. His list is prime numbers between 11 and 100 where the first digit is larger than the second digit. The first three numbers in his list are as follows:

31, 41, 43, ...

What is the fourth number in Santosh's list?

A 47   B 61   C 51   D 53   E 45

End of test

CGP

11+ Practice Paper

Set B: Paper 1
Verbal Skills

For the GL Buckinghamshire Transfer Test

Read the following:

Do not open this booklet or start the test until you are told to do so.

1. This is a multiple-choice test. You will have around one hour to complete this paper, including the practice questions and reading time.

2. There are 2 sections in this test — English and Verbal Reasoning.
   You will have 25 minutes to complete the first section, which contains 30 questions.
   You will have 20 minutes to complete the second section, which contains 25 questions.

3. Each section starts with some examples showing you how to answer the questions.
   For each section, you will have 5 minutes to read the examples and answer some practice questions.

4. You should mark your answer to each question in pencil on the separate answer sheet.

5. Unless told otherwise, you should only mark one answer for each question.
   To mark your answer, draw a straight line through the rectangle next to the option you have chosen. If you make a mistake, rub it out and mark your new answer clearly.

6. Make sure you keep your place on the answer sheet and mark your answer in the box that has the same number as the question.

7. Do as many questions as you can. If you get stuck on a question, choose the answer that you think is most likely to be correct, then move on to the next question.

8. You should do any rough working on a separate piece of paper.

Work carefully, but go as quickly as you can.

Exam set ELPCE3 © CGP 2019

Section 1: English

Example and Practice Questions

You have **5 minutes** to complete practice questions P1 to P3. Read each example carefully before attempting to answer the practice question.

Dick Turpin

There are hundreds of romantic stories about highwaymen — masked men who galloped across olden-day Britain on horseback, ambushing wealthy travellers. One such much-heroicised highwayman is Dick Turpin, whose true story is much more grisly than legend tells.

5   Born in 1705 into humble circumstances, Dick Turpin grew up in Essex. He is thought to have had little education and followed in the footsteps of his father to become a butcher.

After opening his own butcher's shop on the outskirts of London, Turpin started assisting a group of deer poachers active in the early 1730s known as the Essex Gang.

Answer these questions about the text. You can refer back to the text if you need to.
Pick the best answer and mark its letter on your answer sheet.

Example

How are the stories told about highwaymen different to reality?

    A   Stories told nowadays are love stories.
    B   Today's stories describe highwaymen as bad characters.
    C   Gory details are often omitted from stories about highwaymen.
    D   Stories told nowadays are more interesting than the reality.
    E   Highwaymen are described as criminals in modern stories.

Answer

    C   *The passage says that the true story of one famous highwayman is "much more grisly" than the made-up story.*

Try the practice question below.

P1   What is the most likely reason why Dick Turpin set up his own butcher's shop?

    A   He didn't spend much time at school.
    B   He learnt how to be a butcher through the family business.
    C   He had always dreamed of being a butcher.
    D   He received money from gangs to help him buy a shop.
    E   Butchers' shops were popular in suburban London.

The sentences below contain some spelling mistakes. Each line has either one mistake or no mistake. For each line, work out which group of words contains a mistake and mark the letter on your answer sheet. Mark N if there is no mistake.

Example

After countless years of disagreements, the former adverseries decided to reconcile.
| A | B | C | D | N |

Answer

C 'adverseries' should be 'adversaries'.

Try the practice question below.

P2 My teacher is always concerned with adressing the worst behaviour.
| A | B | C | D | N |

Choose the word which completes each passage correctly. Each passage needs to make sense and be written in correct English. Pick one of the five options and mark the letter on your answer sheet.

Example

According to the rule book, **however whichever whatever whoever whom**
| A | B | C | D | E |

won the previous round of the game selects who has to go first in this round.

Answer

D 'whoever' is the only word that makes sense with the rest of the sentence.

Try the practice question below.

I was surprised to learn that the new television series is actually

P3 adapted **on with from by in** a novel by my favourite writer.
A B C D E

End of Practice Questions

Do not go on until you are told to

Read this passage carefully and answer the questions that follow.
You have **25 minutes** to complete this section, which contains 30 questions.

An abridged extract from 'The Water-Babies'

Now you must know that all the things under the water talk; and Tom soon learned to understand them and talk to them; so that he might have had very pleasant company if he had only been a good boy. But I am sorry to say, he was too like some other little boys, very fond of hunting and tormenting creatures for mere sport.

5   One day he found a caddis* and wanted it to peep out of its house: but its house-door was shut. He had never seen a caddis with a house-door before: so what must he do, the meddlesome little fellow, but pull it open. Tom broke to pieces the door; and when he looked in, the caddis poked out her head. But when Tom spoke to her she could not answer; for her mouth and face were tight tied up in a new night-cap of neat pink skin. However, if she didn't answer, all
10   the other caddises did; for they held up their hands and shrieked: "Oh, you nasty horrid boy; there you are at it again! And she had just laid herself up for a fortnight's sleep; and now you have broken her door, and she can't mend it because her mouth is tied up for a fortnight. Who sent you here to worry us out of our lives?"

So Tom swam away. He was very much ashamed of himself, and felt all the naughtier; as little
15   boys do when they have done wrong and won't say so. Under a bank he saw a very ugly dirty creature sitting, about half as big as himself; which had six legs, and a big stomach, and a most ridiculous head with two great eyes and a face just like a donkey's.

"Oh," said Tom, "you are an ugly fellow to be sure!" and he began making faces at him, when, out popped a long arm with a pair of pincers at the end of it, and caught Tom by the nose.
20   "Yah, ah! Oh, let me go!" cried Tom.

"Then let me go," said the creature. "I want to be quiet. I want to split."

Tom promised to let him alone, and he let go.

"Why do you want to split?" said Tom.

"Because my brothers and sisters have all split, and turned into beautiful creatures with wings;
25   and I want to split too. Don't speak to me. I am sure I shall split. I will split!"

Tom stood still, and watched him. And he swelled himself, and puffed, and stretched himself out stiff, and at last he opened all down his back, and then up to the top of his head.

And out of his inside came the most slender, elegant, soft creature: but very pale and weak. It moved its legs very feebly; and looked about it half ashamed, like a girl when she goes for the first
30   time into a ballroom; and then it began walking slowly up a grass stem to the top of the water.

As the creature sat in the warm bright sun, a wonderful change came over it. It grew strong and firm; the most lovely colours began to show on its body; out of its back rose four great wings; and its eyes grew so large that they filled all its head, and shone like ten thousand diamonds.

"Oh, you beautiful creature!" said Tom; and he put out his hand to catch it.
35   But the thing whirred up into the air, and hung poised on its wings a moment, and then settled down again by Tom quite fearless.

"No!" it said, "you cannot catch me. I am a dragon-fly now, the king of all the flies!"

by Charles Kingsley

*caddis — *a moth-like creature that lays eggs underwater*

Answer these questions about the text. You can refer back to the text if you need to.
Pick the best answer and mark its letter on your answer sheet.

1 According to the passage, which of the following statements about Tom is true?

- **A** He doesn't like talking to animals.
- **B** He has always known how to talk to animals.
- **C** Other little boys are a bad influence on him.
- **D** He mistreats animals.
- **E** He doesn't like being under the water.

2 Why does Tom open the caddis' house-door?

- **A** He wanted to talk to the caddis.
- **B** He was curious.
- **C** He had nothing better to do.
- **D** He doesn't like caddises.
- **E** He had always wanted to see a caddis with a house-door.

3 Why doesn't the caddis speak to Tom?

- **A** She doesn't like him.
- **B** She was too sleepy.
- **C** She doesn't know how to speak.
- **D** She has her mouth sealed up.
- **E** She was too surprised.

4 Why do you think the caddises say "there you are at it again!" (lines 10-11)?

- **A** They are pleased to see Tom.
- **B** They see Tom at this time every day.
- **C** They know that Tom has caused mischief like this before.
- **D** They want to join in with Tom's mischief.
- **E** They have all met Tom before.

5 How does Tom react to being told off by the caddises?

- **A** He doesn't admit to the caddises that he's done something wrong.
- **B** He refuses to feel bad about what he's done.
- **C** He feels naughtier than he thinks he should.
- **D** He decides to stop tormenting creatures.
- **E** He shouts back at them.

6 The creature says that it wants to "split" (line 21). This means that:

- **A** It wants to leave the water.
- **B** It wants to swim away from Tom.
- **C** It wants to come out of hibernation.
- **D** It wants to leave its family.
- **E** It wants to shed its exoskeleton.

Turn over to the next page

7 Why doesn't the creature want to talk to Tom?

    A It feels offended by Tom.
    B It isn't feeling well.
    C It wants to concentrate.
    D It doesn't know how to talk to Tom.
    E Tom is being too loud.

8 Which of the following statements is false?

    A After transforming, the creature is unwell.
    B After transforming, the creature is self-conscious.
    C After transforming, the creature isn't colourful at first.
    D After transforming, the creature finds it difficult to move.
    E After transforming, the creature looks very different to how it did before.

9 How do you think the dragonfly feels after it has transformed?

    A Appreciated
    B Restless
    C Scornful
    D Disappointed
    E Confident

Answer these questions about the way words and phrases are used in the text.

10 "Under a bank he saw a very ugly dirty creature sitting" (lines 15-16). Which of these words is a preposition?

    A bank
    B creature
    C very
    D Under
    E sitting

11 The word "feebly" (line 29) is an example of which part of speech?

    A Noun
    B Article
    C Adjective
    D Adverb
    E Verb

12 The dragonfly is "half ashamed, like a girl when she goes for the first time into a ballroom" (lines 29-30). This is an example of:

    A a cliché.
    B alliteration.
    C a simile.
    D a metaphor.
    E exaggeration.

Answer these questions about the meaning of words as they are used in the text.

13 Which of these words is closest in meaning to "meddlesome" (line 7)?
- A Interfering
- B Discourteous
- C Scheming
- D Spiteful
- E Troubled

14 Which of these words is closest in meaning to "slender" (line 28)?
- A Confident
- B Suave
- C Lean
- D Nonchalant
- E Graceful

15 What is meant by the phrase "hung poised on its wings" (line 35)?
- A The dragonfly is hovering in the air.
- B The dragonfly is trying to learn how to fly.
- C The dragonfly is holding on to Tom using its wings.
- D The dragonfly is floating down to Tom.
- E The dragonfly is ready to attack Tom with its wings.

Turn over to the next page

This passage contains some spelling mistakes. Each numbered line has either one mistake or no mistake. For each line, work out which group of words contains a mistake, and mark the letter on your answer sheet. Mark N if there is no mistake.

A Mountain Adventure

16 Amanda took a deep breathe before mustering all of her strength to pull herself up
   A / B / C / D / N

17 onto the ledge. Once she felt secure, she scrambled to stand up and admire the
   A / B / C / D / N

18 view. It really was astonishing. The town she had begun her asent from now
   A / B / C / D / N

19 looked like a minature toy set in the distance. She could have spent all day gazing
   A / B / C / D / N

20 over the magnificent valley. Yet she still had a long way to climb to reach the sumit.
   A / B / C / D / N

This passage contains some mistakes involving capital letters and punctuation. Each numbered line has either one mistake or no mistake. For each line, work out which group of words contains a mistake and mark the letter on your answer sheet. Mark N if there is no mistake.

Year Without a Summer

21 Volcanoes are responsible for creating many natural features; rock formations,
   A / B / C / D / N

22 lava flows, and even new islands. However, they can also impact the weather. In 1815,
   A / B / C / D / N

23 a volcanic eruption in indonesia released sulphur dioxide into the atmosphere, causing
   A / B / C / D / N

24 a drop in global temperatures. This triggered strange weather across lots of other
   A / B / C / D / N

25 countries' in 1816, which consequently became known as the year without a summer.
   A / B / C / D / N

For each numbered line, choose the word, or group of words, which completes the passage correctly. The passage needs to make sense and be written in correct English. Pick one of the five options and mark the letter on your answer sheet.

Volunteers Wanted

26 The Moose Forest Nature Park are appealing **for / on / with / out / from** nature lovers
                                                               A   B   C   D   E

27 **which / what / who / whom / whoever** might be able to help with its exciting new
     A   B   C   D   E

28 environmental programme. There are many roles on **available / free / offer / open / vacant**
                                                               A   B   C   D   E

so there should be something for everyone. They are looking for someone with gardening

29 experience to help plant new trees to replace **them / they / it / who / those** that burnt
                                                                A   B   C   D   E

30 down in the forest fire last year. They are also looking **after / for / out / in / about** experienced
                                                                              A   B   C   D   E

outdoor enthusiasts to be guides on their nature walks.

End of Section 1

Do not go on until you are told to

Section 2: Verbal Reasoning

Example and Practice Questions

You have **5 minutes** to complete practice questions P1 to P6. Read the examples carefully and mark your answers to the practice questions on the answer sheet.

Find **two** words, one from each set of brackets, that have the most **opposite** meaning. Mark **both** words on the answer sheet.

Example (good tasty sweet) (torn dirty bad)

        A good   **X** torn
        B tasty   **Y** dirty
        C sweet   **Z** bad

Answer **good** and **bad**
'good' means 'of a high quality or standard', whereas 'bad' means 'of a low quality or standard'.

Try the practice question below.

P1 (vulnerable frail puny) (hearty gleeful capable)

        A vulnerable   **X** hearty
        B frail   **Y** gleeful
        C puny   **Z** capable

The number codes for three of these four words are listed in a random order. Work out the code to answer the question.

Example

        TIME   NEAT   MINE   MEAN
        1463   2413   1356

Find the code for the word **TIME**.

    A 2413   **B** 1463   **C** 6352   **D** 2143   **E** 6335

Answer **2413** T = 2, I = 4, M = 1, E = 3

Try the practice question below.

        FAST   STAR   RACE   SEAT
        2468   3841   7431

P2 Find the code for the word **STAR**.

    A 7234   **B** 3841   **C** 6841   **D** 3142   **E** 7431

Read the information carefully, then use it to answer the question that follows.

Example

> Kemal, Maya, Luke, Erica and Sajid all took some books out of the school library. Everyone except Luke chose a history book. Luke was the only one who chose a book of poetry. Nobody except Maya and Sajid chose a book about trains. Erica, Kemal and Maya all chose recipe books.
> The only child who did not choose a story book was Sajid.
>
> Which child chose the **most** books?
>
> **A** Kemal   **B** Maya   **C** Luke   **D** Erica   **E** Sajid

Answer   Maya   *Maya chose four books — a history book, a book about trains, a recipe book and a story book.*

Try the practice question below.

P3 Maisie, Aminah, Tony, Charlotte and Dan did an Easter egg hunt for different coloured eggs. Everyone except Tony found a blue egg. Maisie was the only child to find a green egg. Nobody found a red egg apart from Aminah.
Everyone except Aminah and Dan found a pink egg.
Tony and Aminah were the only ones to find a yellow egg.

Which child found the **fewest** eggs?

    A Maisie   **B** Aminah   **C** Tony   **D** Charlotte   **E** Dan

---

Remove one letter from the first word and add it to the second word to make two new words. Do not change the order of the other letters. Mark the letter that moves on the answer sheet.

Example   peach   ant

    A p   **B** e   **C** a   **D** c   **E** h

Answer   p   *The new words are **each** and **pant**.*

Try the practice question below.

P4 drawn   tip

    A d   **B** r   **C** a   **D** w   **E** n

Turn over to the next page

Each letter stands for a number. Work out the answer to each sum and find its letter. Mark that letter on the answer sheet.

Example A = 3, B = 4, C = 7, D = 10, E = 11

   C + A = (?)

   A A   **B** B   **C** C   **D** D   **E** E

Answer D   *7 + 3 = 10*

Try the practice question below.

P5 A = 4, B = 6, C = 3, D = 9, E = 12

   D - C = (?)

   A A   **B** B   **C** C   **D** D   **E** E

Find the letter that will finish the first word and start the second word of each pair. The same letter must be used for both pairs.

Example not (?) gg   rip (?) ven

   A a   **B** e   **C** d   **D** k   **E** g

Answer e   *The new words are 'note', 'egg', 'ripe' and 'even'.*

Try the practice question below.

P6 stee (?) eel   sho (?) ark

   A t   **B** p   **C** r   **D** d   **E** l

End of Practice Questions

Do not go on until you are told to

You have **20 minutes** to complete this section, which contains 25 questions.

Find **two** words, one from each set of brackets, that have the most **opposite** meaning.
Mark **both** words on the answer sheet.

Example (good tasty sweet)   (torn dirty bad)

          A good   X torn
          B tasty   Y dirty
          C sweet   Z bad

Answer good bad

1. (overbearing reckless calm)   (reasonable polite meek)
    A overbearing
    B reckless
    C calm
    X reasonable
    Y polite
    Z meek

2. (rude tender naive)   (courteous ignorant obliging)
    A rude
    B tender
    C naive
    X courteous
    Y ignorant
    Z obliging

3. (exchange collection unity)   (dissection division displacement)
    A exchange
    B collection
    C unity
    X dissection
    Y division
    Z displacement

4. (stop arrest punish)   (liberate extract disentangle)
    A stop
    B arrest
    C punish
    X liberate
    Y extract
    Z disentangle

5. (recommend provide reward)   (criticise penalise argue)
    A recommend
    B provide
    C reward
    X criticise
    Y penalise
    Z argue

Turn over to the next page

The number codes for three of these four words are listed in a random order.
Work out the code to answer the questions.

CARE   CRAB   BEAR   NAME

2135   6513   7145

6 Find the code for the word **CRAB**.
A 7145   B 3135   C 2316   D 6513   E 2135

7 Find the code for the word **BEAM**.
A 6132   B 3415   C 2453   D 1273   E 6514

8 Find the word that has the number code **4135**.
A MANE   B MARE   C RACE   D AREA   E CRAM

Read the information carefully, then use it to answer the question that follows.

9 Diana, Alastair, Rachel, Jenny and Andrew are at the ice cream parlour.
Everyone starts with a scoop of vanilla except for Alastair. Andrew and Alastair both have a scoop of raspberry and a scoop of strawberry. Jenny, Andrew and Diana each have one scoop of chocolate. Rachel and Jenny both have an extra scoop of vanilla.

Which child has the **most** scoops?

A Diana   B Alastair   C Rachel   D Jenny   E Andrew

10 Different numbers of trains stop at the local station on different days, with no trains at the weekend. Monday has one fewer train than Thursday. There are more trains on Monday than on Tuesday. Wednesday has the largest number of trains. Thursday and Friday have the same number of trains.

Which day has the **smallest** number of trains?

A Monday   B Tuesday   C Wednesday   D Thursday   E Friday

Remove one letter from the first word and add it to the second word to make two new words. Do not change the order of the other letters. Mark the letter that moves on the answer sheet.

Example	peach	ant			
	A p	**B** e	**C** a	**D** c	**E** h
Answer	p (the new words are **each** and **pant**)				

11 coast his
 A c **B** o **C** a **D** s **E** t

12 short fee
 A s **B** h **C** o **D** r **E** t

13 range wet
 A r **B** a **C** n **D** g **E** e

14 below cod
 A b **B** e **C** l **D** o **E** w

15 stage sea
 A s **B** t **C** a **D** g **E** e

Each letter stands for a number. Work out the answer to each sum and find its letter. Mark that letter on the answer sheet.

Example A = 3, B = 4, C = 7, D = 10, E = 11

C + A = (?)

 A A **B** B **C** C **D** D **E** E

Answer D

16 A = 3, B = 4, C = 5, D = 6, E = 9
 E − C = (?)
 A A **B** B **C** C **D** D **E** E

17 A = 2, B = 3, C = 4, D = 5, E = 6
 A + D − B = (?)
 A A **B** B **C** C **D** D **E** E

Turn over to the next page

18 A = 2, B = 4, C = 6, D = 8, E = 10
D ÷ A + C = (?)

A A **B** B **C** C **D** D **E** E

19 A = 3, B = 4, C = 7, D = 8, E = 11
A × B − D = (?)

A A **B** B **C** C **D** D **E** E

20 A = 3, B = 4, C = 6, D = 9, E = 12
E ÷ B × A = (?)

A A **B** B **C** C **D** D **E** E

Find the letter that will finish the first word and start the second word of each pair.
The same letter must be used for both pairs.

Example	not (?) gg	rip (?) ven				
	A a	**B** e	**C** d	**D** k	**E** g
Answer	e					

21 kin (?) row   son (?) ate
A d **B** g **C** c **D** p **E** s

22 war (?) act   ram (?) age
A m **B** f **C** p **D** d **E** e

23 gas (?) eel   wit (?) and
A p **B** f **C** s **D** l **E** h

24 bee (?) our   scar (?) ail
A m **B** n **C** r **D** f **E** d

25 plea (?) own   see (?) ash
A d **B** n **C** t **D** k **E** p

End of test

CGP

11+ Practice Paper

Set B: Paper 2
Mathematical & Non-Verbal Skills

For the GL Buckinghamshire Transfer Test

Read the following:

Do not open this booklet or start the test until you are told to do so.

1. This is a multiple-choice test. You will have around one hour to complete this paper, including the practice questions and reading time.

2. There are 2 sections in this test — Non-Verbal & Spatial Reasoning and Maths.

3. Section 1 — Non-Verbal & Spatial Reasoning is divided into smaller subsections. Each subsection starts with some examples showing you how to answer the questions. You will be given time at the start of each subsection to complete the practice questions. You will then have 5 minutes to complete each subsection.

4. You will have 5 minutes to complete the practice questions at the start of Section 2 — Maths. You will then have 25 minutes to complete the second section, which contains 23 questions.

5. You should mark your answer to each question in pencil on the separate answer sheet.

6. You should only mark one answer for each question. To mark your answer, draw a straight line through the rectangle next to the option you have chosen. If you make a mistake, rub it out and mark your new answer clearly.

7. Make sure you keep your place on the answer sheet and mark your answer in the box that has the same number as the question.

8. Do as many questions as you can. If you get stuck on a question, choose the answer that you think is most likely to be correct, then move on to the next question.

9. You should do any rough working on a separate piece of paper.

Work carefully, but go as quickly as you can.

Exam set ELPCE3

Section 1: Non-Verbal & Spatial Reasoning

Example and Practice Questions

On the left of the questions below there are three figures that are like each other in some way. On the right there are five more figures. Find the figure on the right which is **most like** those on the left. **Mark its letter** on the **answer sheet**.

Example

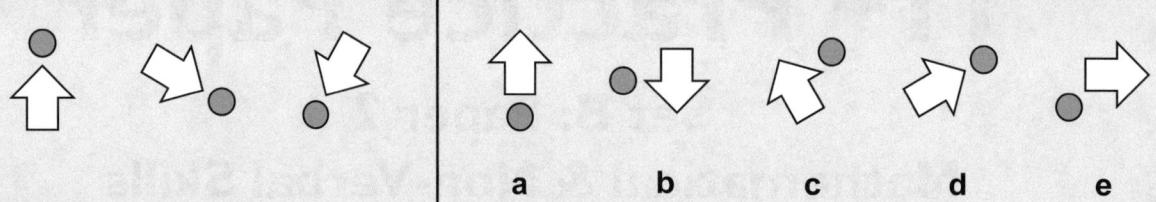

Answer: d *In all figures, the arrow must be pointing towards the grey circle.*

Try these two practice questions below:

P1

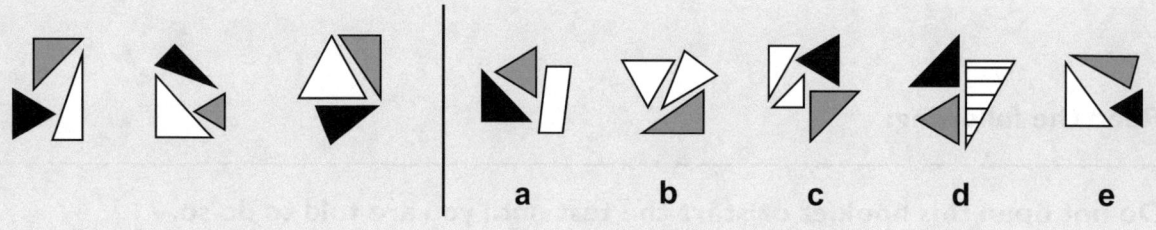

P2

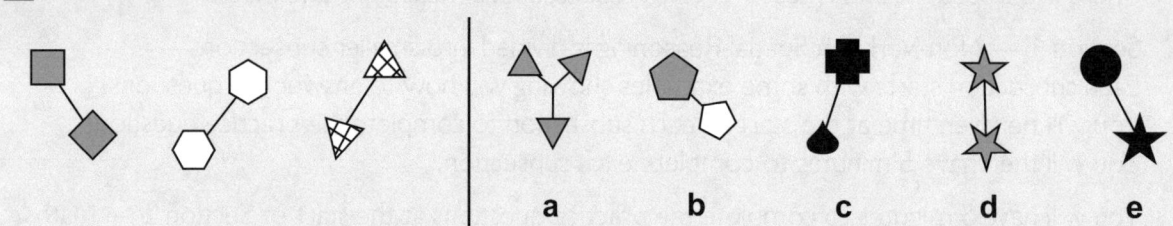

End of Practice Questions. Do not go on until you are told to.

You have **5 minutes** to complete this subsection, which contains 7 questions.

1

   |

a   b   c   d   e

Now go to the next question

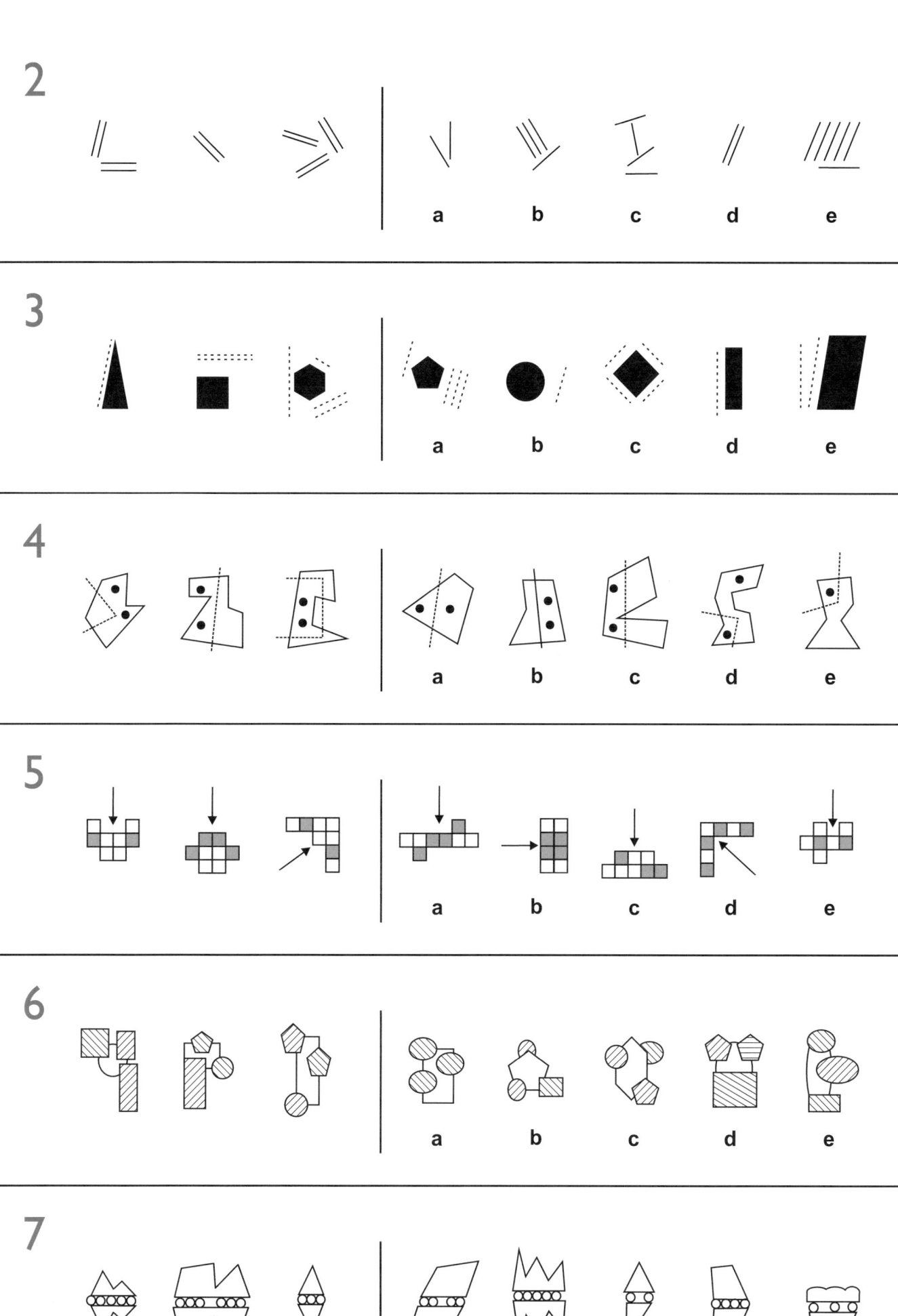

Example and Practice Questions

Each question has some shapes on the left with code letters that describe them. You need to work out what the code letters mean. There is then a shape on its own next to a choice of five codes. Work out which code describes this shape. **Mark its letter** on the **answer sheet**.

Example

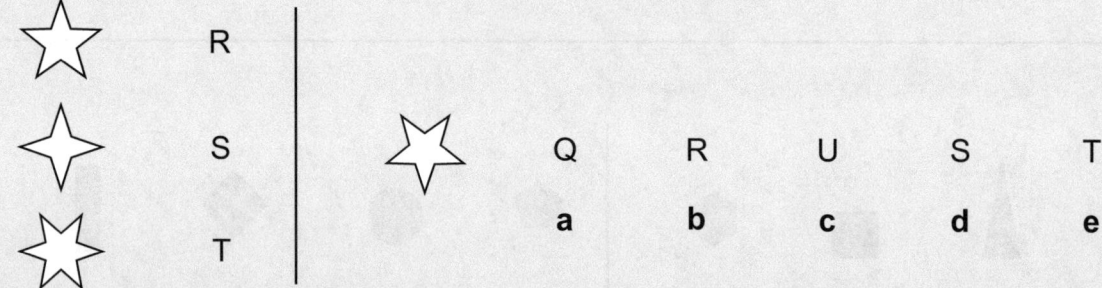

Answer: b *The four-pointed star has the code letter **S**, the five-pointed star has the code letter **R**, and the six-pointed star has the code letter **T**. The new shape is a five-pointed star, so the code must be **R** and the answer is **b**.*

Try the two practice questions below. **Each question has a different code.**

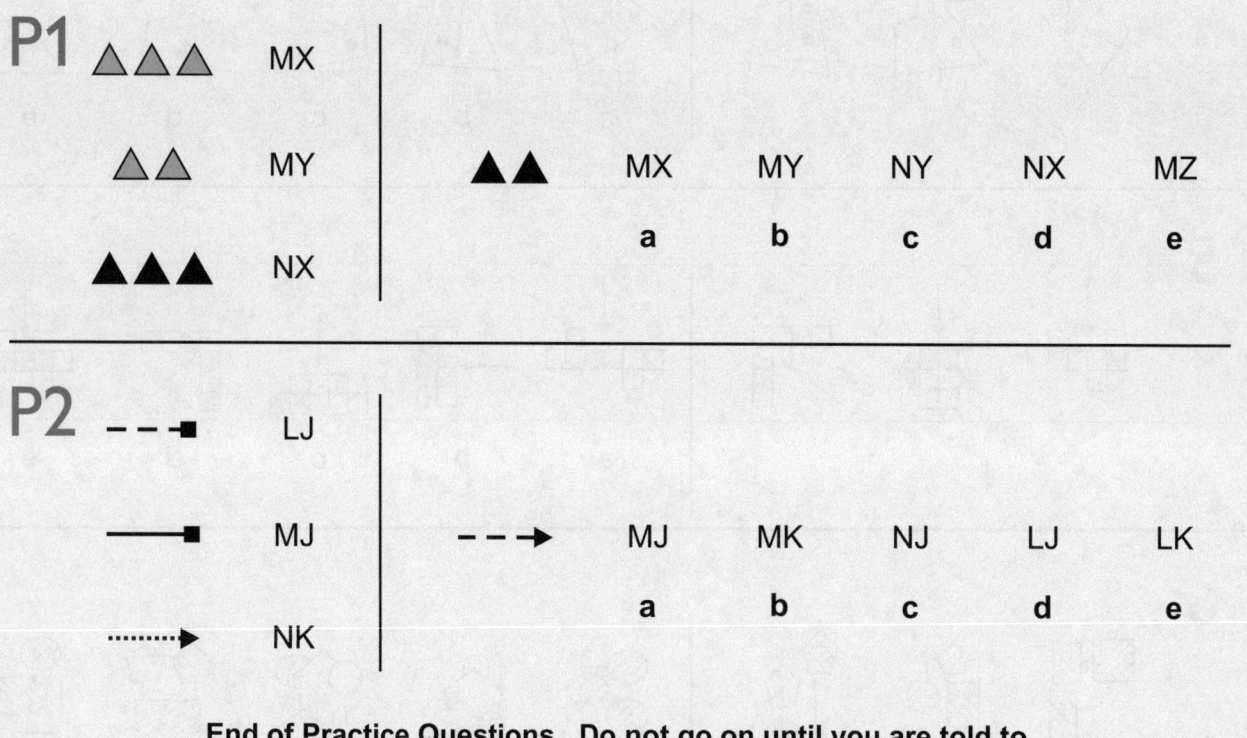

End of Practice Questions. Do not go on until you are told to.

You have **5 minutes** to complete this subsection, which contains 7 questions.

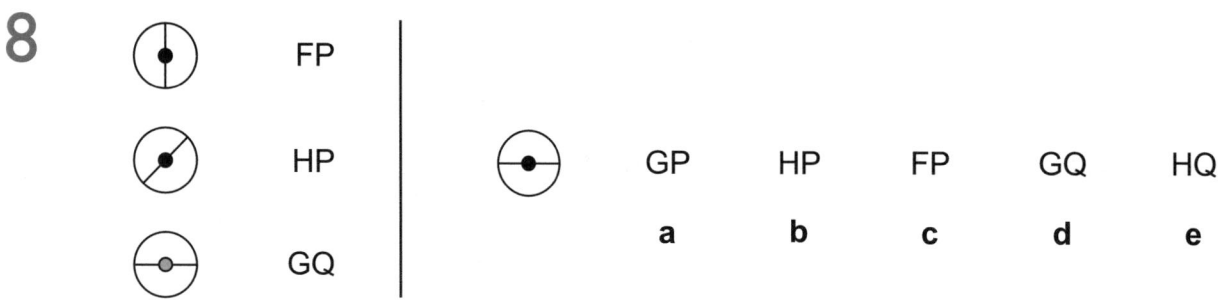

Now go to the next question

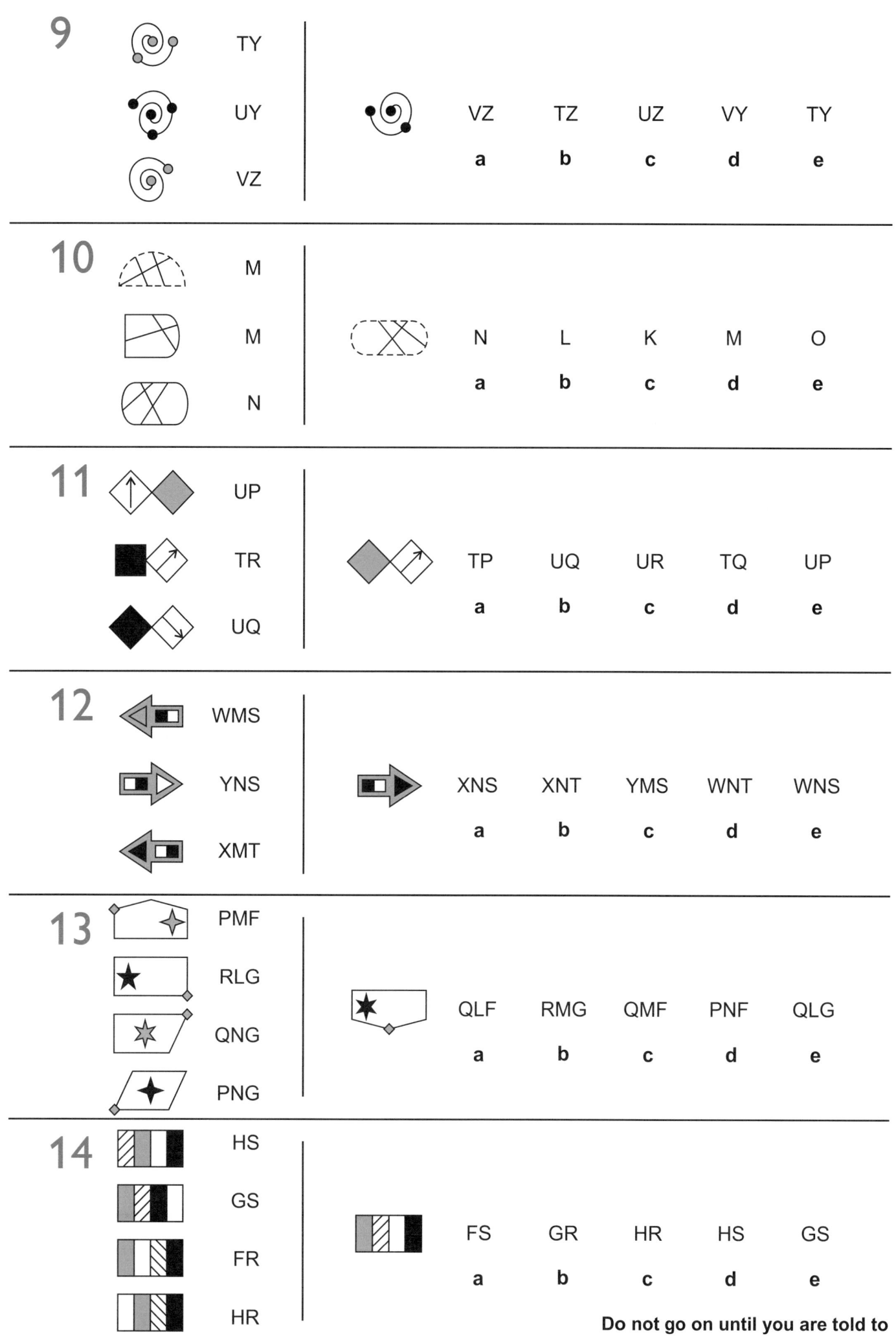

Example and Practice Questions

Work out which 3D figure to the left of the line has been rotated to make the new 3D figure to the right of the line. **Mark its letter** on the **answer sheet**.

Example

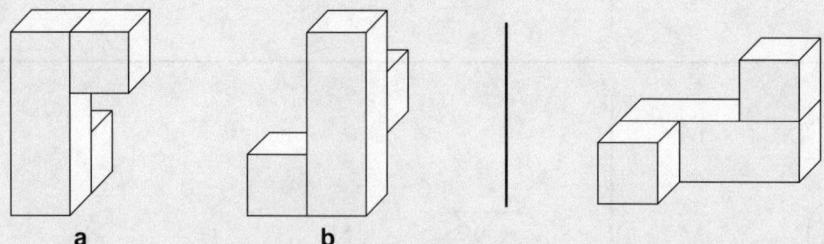

Answer: a *Shape a has been rotated 90 degrees towards you, top-to-bottom. It has then been rotated 90 degrees right-to-left.*

Try these two practice questions below:

Work out which 3D figures (a, b, c, d, e or f) have been rotated to make the new 3D figures P1 and P2.

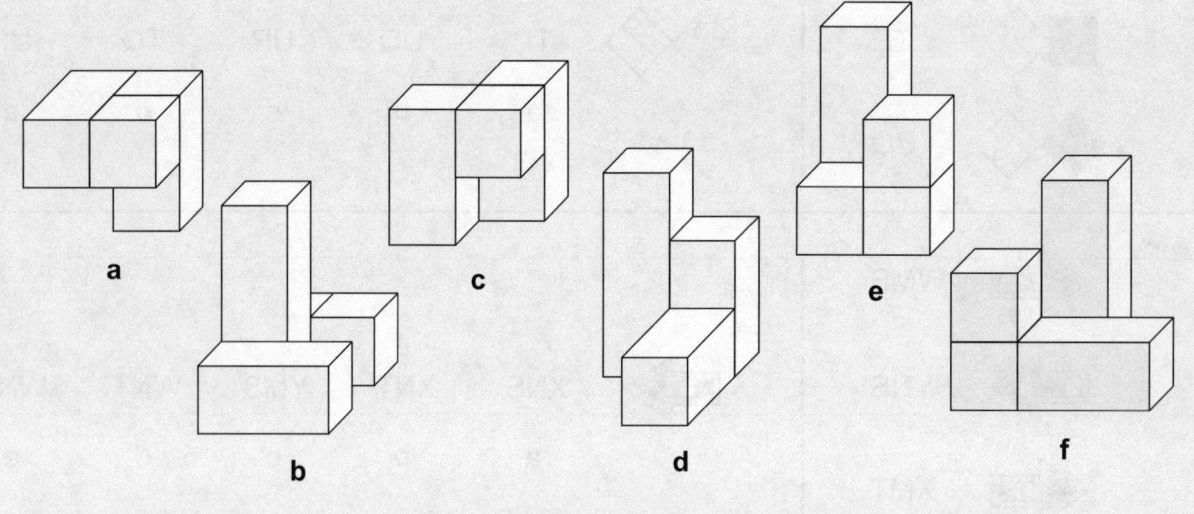

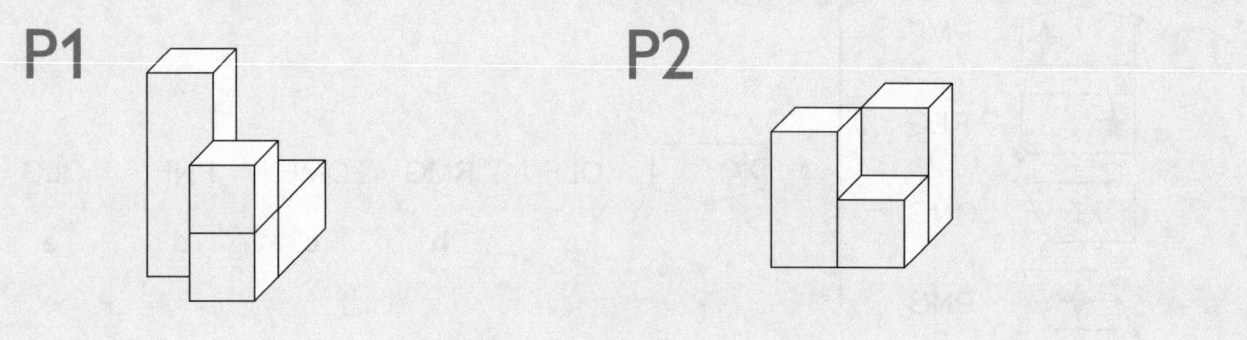

End of Practice Questions

Do not go on until you are told to

You have **5 minutes** to complete this subsection, which contains 6 questions.

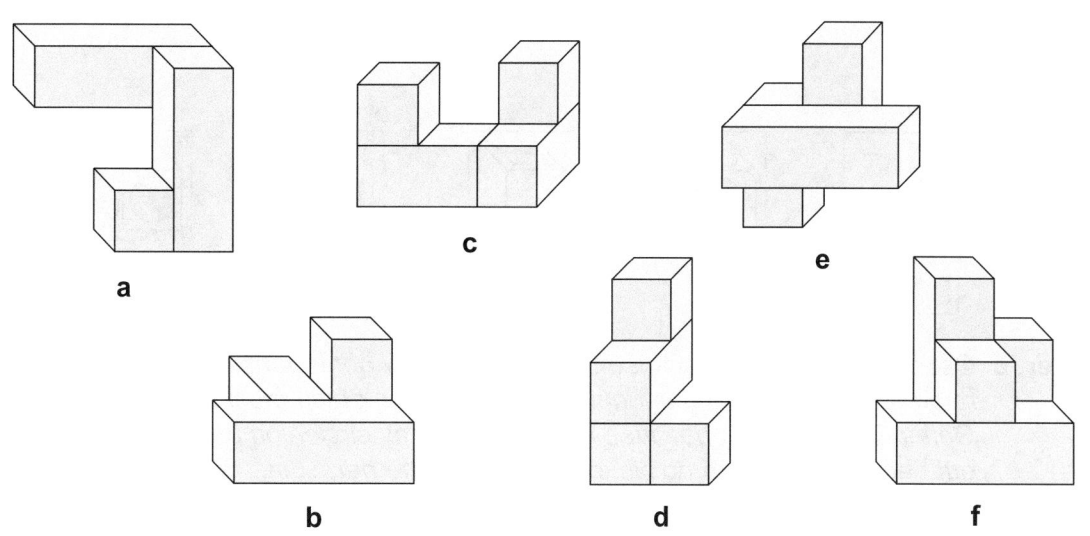

---

15 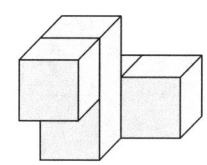   16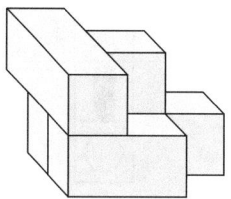

---

17 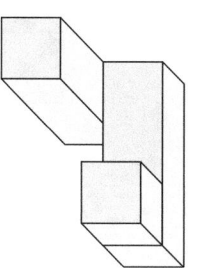   18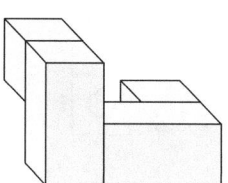

---

19 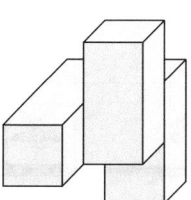   20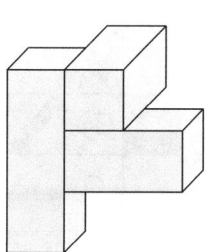

Do not go on until you are told to

Example and Practice Questions

Work out which of the five cubes can be made from the net. **Mark its letter** on the **answer sheet**.

Example

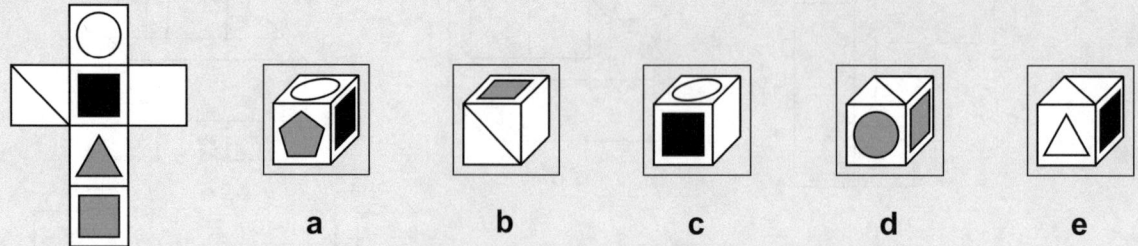

Answer: c Option A is ruled out because there are no grey pentagons on the net. Option B is ruled out because the diagonal line and the blank face must be on opposite sides. Option D is ruled out because there are no grey circles on the net. Option E is ruled out because there are no white triangles on the net.

Try these two practice questions below:

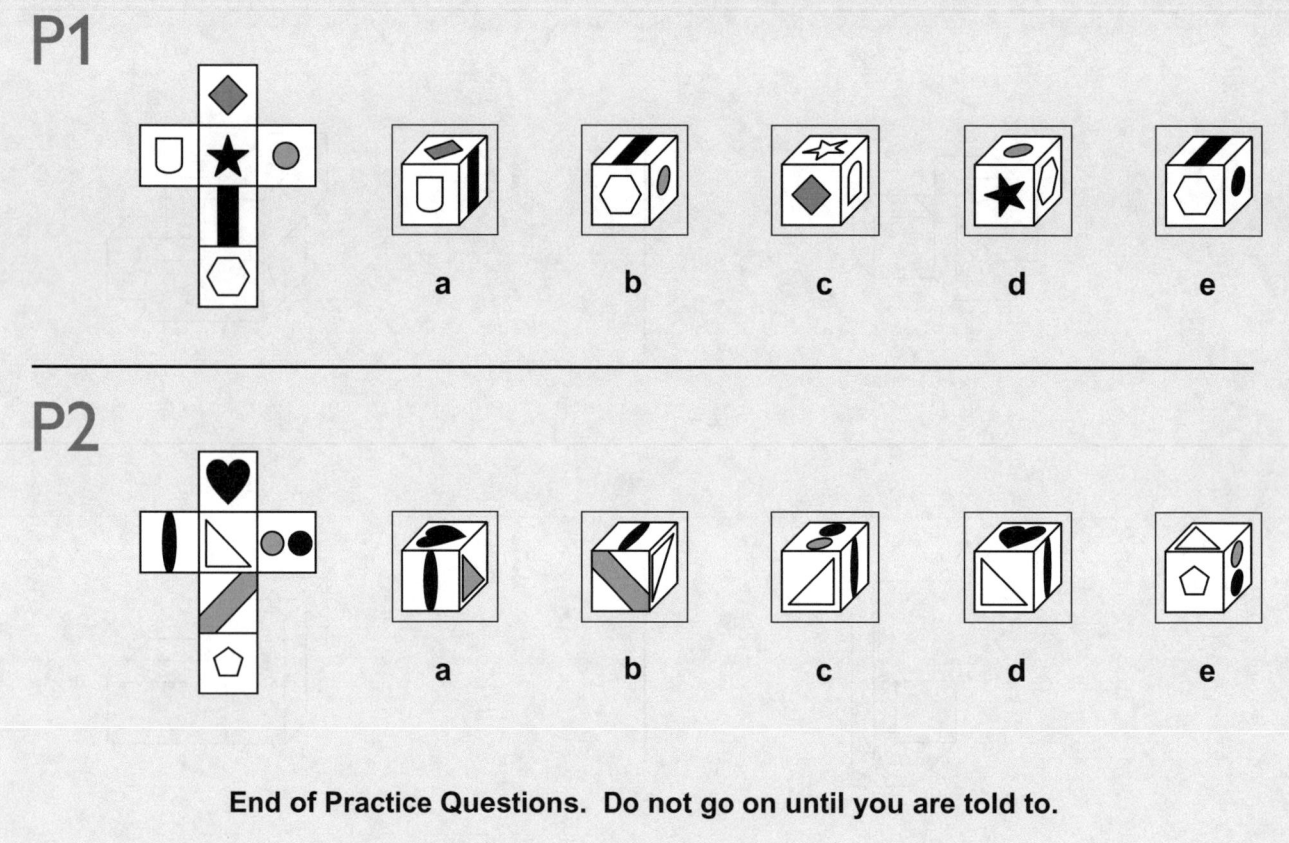

End of Practice Questions. Do not go on until you are told to.

You have **5 minutes** to complete this subsection, which contains 7 questions.

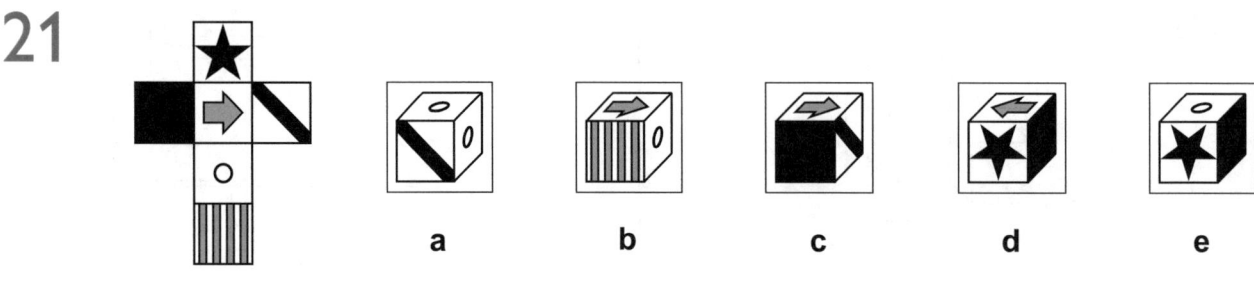

Now go to the next question

22

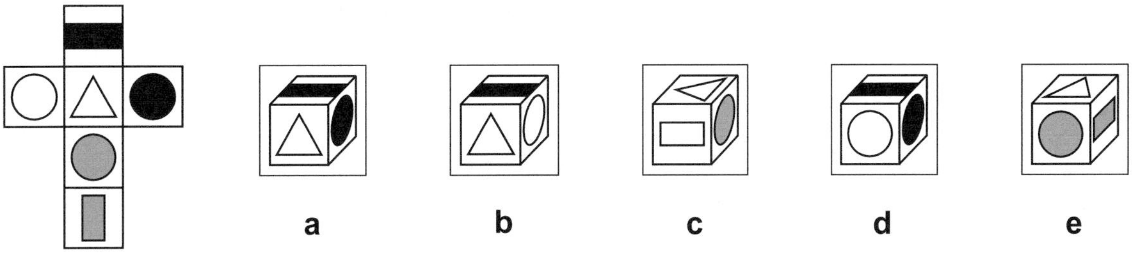

23

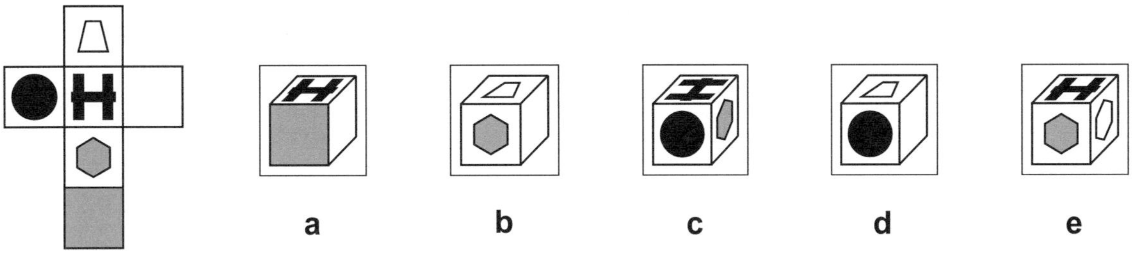

24

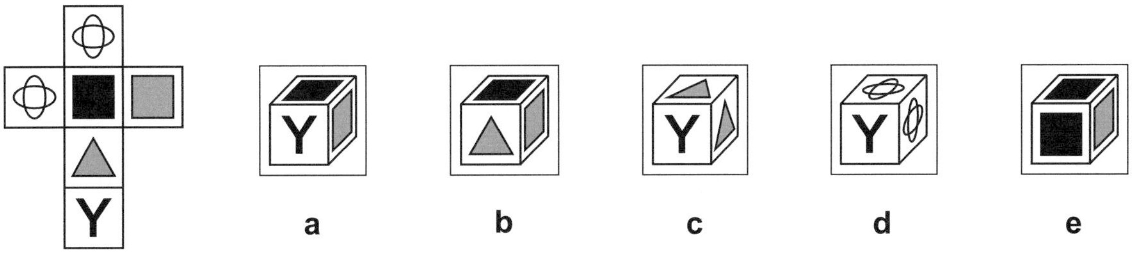

25

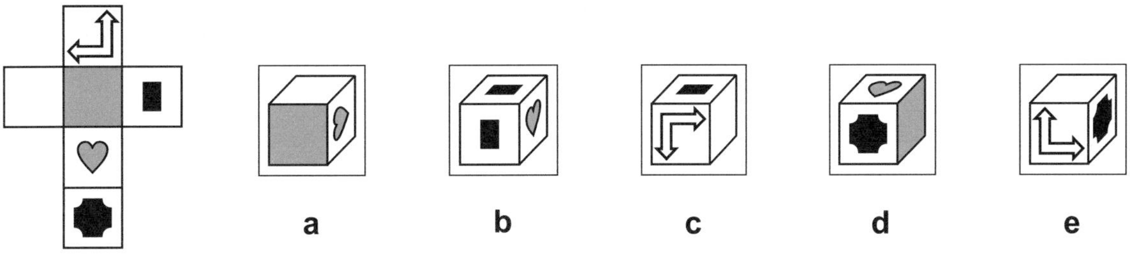

26

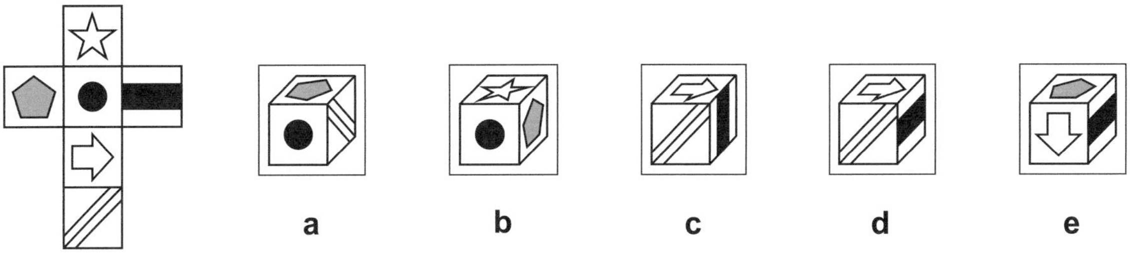

27

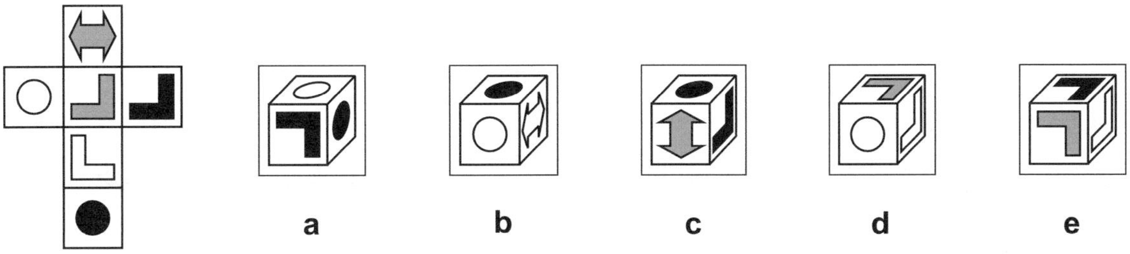

End of Section 1

Do not go on until you are told to

Section 2: Maths

Example and Practice Questions

You have **5 minutes** to complete practice questions P1 to P3.
Read the example carefully before attempting to answer the practice questions.

Example

Michelle bought a book for £6.99 and a pen for 76p.
How much did she spend?

A £7.75   B £6.23   C £7.76   D £8.99   E £8.76

Answer

£7.75   *Convert 76p to pounds so it's £0.76. Michelle spent £6.99 + £0.76 so in total she spent £7.75.*

Try the practice questions below:

P1 Which of these numbers can be multiplied by 4 to get 212?

   A 43   B 52   C 53   D 63   E 64

P2 Tom's Tiles is a company that makes small ceramic tiles. They store the tiles in small cuboid boxes. The shape of each box is the same as the one in the diagram below.

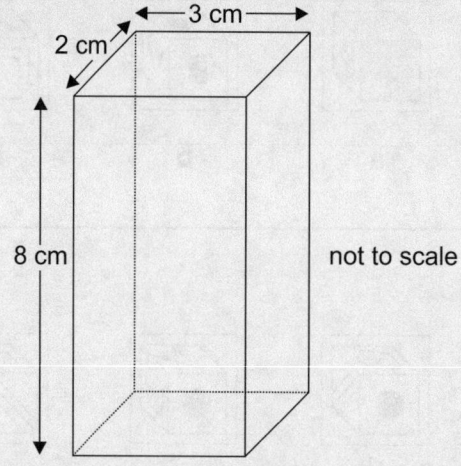

not to scale

What is the volume of the box?

   A 64 cm³   B 44 cm³   C 26 cm³   D 48 cm³   E 32 cm³

P3 Which of the following could be the capacity of a bottle of water sold in a supermarket?

   A 1 millilitre   B 10 millilitres   C 1 litre   D 100 litres   E 0.01 litres

End of Practice Questions

Do not go on until you are told to

The following questions will test your mathematical skills.
You will have **25 minutes** to complete this section, which contains 23 questions.

1 Saba is painting her house using a ladder.
She puts the ladder so it leans against the wall, as shown in the diagram.

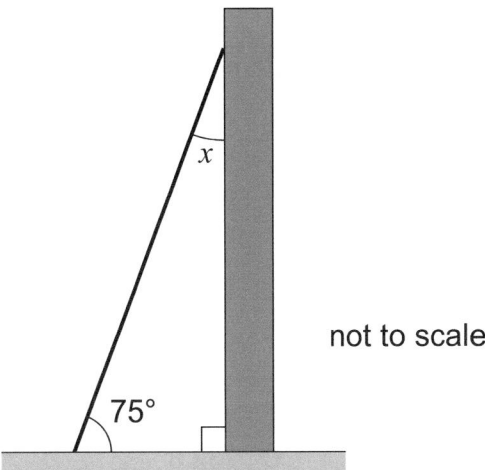

not to scale

What is the size of angle x?

A 75° B 165° C 25° D 105° E 15°

2 A lorry's milometer shows the following number.

57692

What is this number rounded to the nearest thousand?

A 58 000 B 57 000 C 59 000 D 57 500 E 60 000

3 Around 71% of the Earth's surface is covered by water.
Which of the following is closest to showing that percentage as a fraction?

A ½ B ⅘ C ¾ D ¼ E ⁶⁄₁₀

4 Amrita thinks of a number. She divides it by 3, then adds 5.
Her answer is 14. What was Amrita's original number?

A 57 B 27 C 55 D 3 E 29

5 Joni is a taxi driver. She picks a passenger up at an office, then is asked to take the passenger to the bank and then to the restaurant. The restaurant is 15 km away from the office. The bank is on the way to the restaurant and is 4500 m away from the office. What is the distance between the bank and the restaurant?

A 11 500 m B 30 km C 9 km D 4500 m E 10.5 km

Turn over to the next page

6 Blair runs around a rectangular race track, shown below.

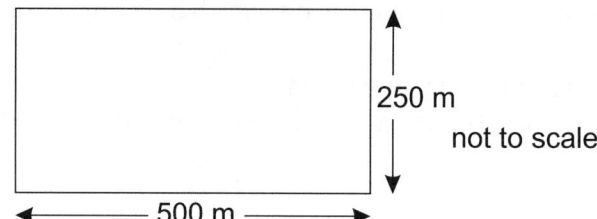

Blair does two laps of the track. How far does she travel?

A 1.5 km   B 2.5 km   C 0.75 km   D 3 km   E 1.25 km

7 458 × 0.16 = 73.28

What is 458 × 1.6?

A 7.328   B 7328   C 732.8   D 7.238   E 0.7328

8 Abbey, Buddy, Candy and Derek are racing drones around a town. The drones complete twenty races in total. Abbey won three more races than Candy. Candy won six times as many races as Buddy. Abbey won nine races. How many races did Derek win?

A 6   B 3   C 5   D 4   E 7

9 A group of students are practising the triple jump. They each record their shortest jump and their longest jump. Their results are shown in the graph below.

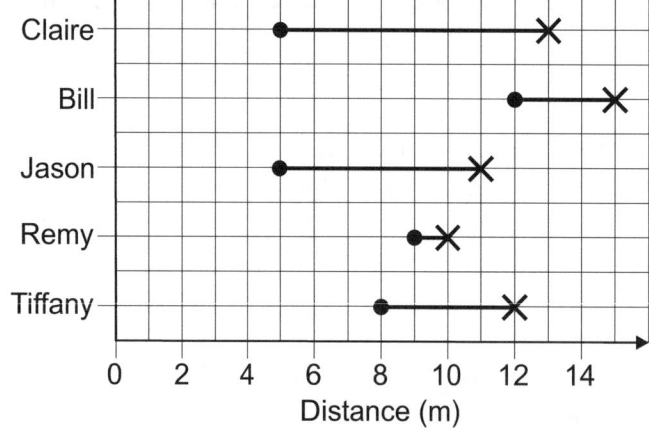
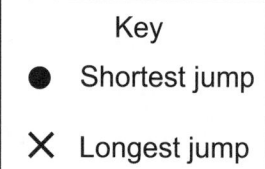

Who had the smallest difference between their longest jump and their shortest jump?

A Claire   B Bill   C Jason   D Remy   E Tiffany

10 Alfred cycles from Amblewick to Winderside. The distance between Amblewick and Winderside is 32 km, and Alfred cycles at the same speed for the whole journey. If Alfred leaves Amblewick at 13:00 and it takes him 14 minutes to travel 4 km, what time does he arrive in Winderside?

A 15:08   B 14:38   C 13:56   D 15:12   E 14:52

11 Apriya and Ben are go-karting around a race track. They each complete 3 laps. Apriya starts the race 5 metres ahead of Ben. With every lap, Apriya doubles his lead over Ben and then adds a further 2 metres per lap to his lead. How far ahead of Ben is Apriya when he has completed 3 laps?

A 54 m   B 12 m   C 30 m   D 62 m   E 64 m

12 Raheem uses a pencil to shade in a shape on a piece of 1 cm² squared paper, shown below. The piece of paper has 100 squares.

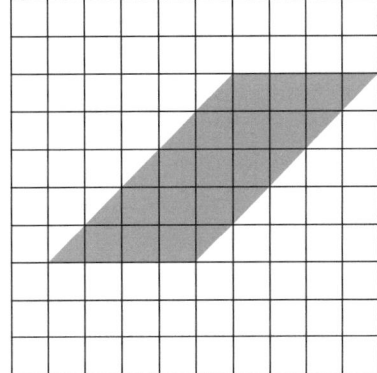

What fraction of the paper is shaded?

A $\frac{1}{5}$ B $\frac{3}{10}$ C $\frac{1}{2}$ D $\frac{8}{10}$ E $\frac{2}{5}$

13 Umair and Betty own a bakery. Umair and Betty make all of the cakes for the bakery. The number of cakes they made this week is displayed in the bar chart below.

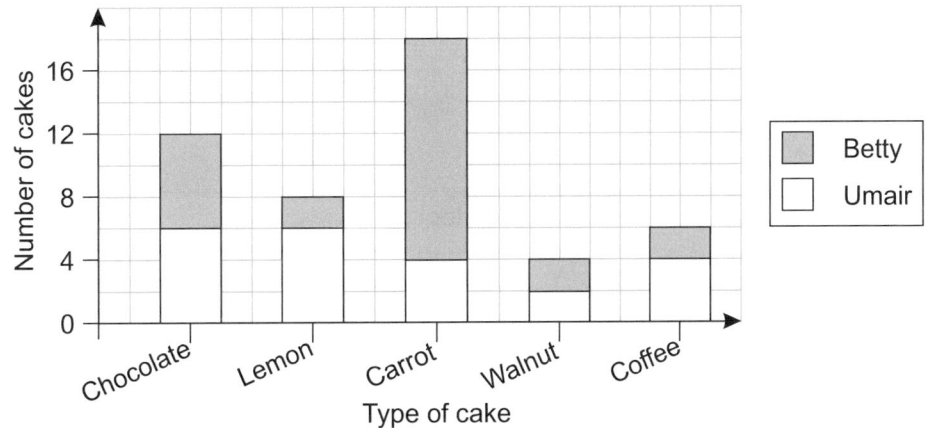

The bakery lists the cakes on its noticeboard in the order of how many were made in total that week. Which cake is in the middle of the list this week?

A Walnut   B Carrot   C Lemon   D Chocolate   E Coffee

14 The *n*th number in a sequence is 5*n* + 2. What is the 10th number in this sequence?

A 70 **B** 10 **C** 52 **D** 17 **E** 47

15 Max is rowing on a lake. He rows over to Island A, which is shown on the grid below.

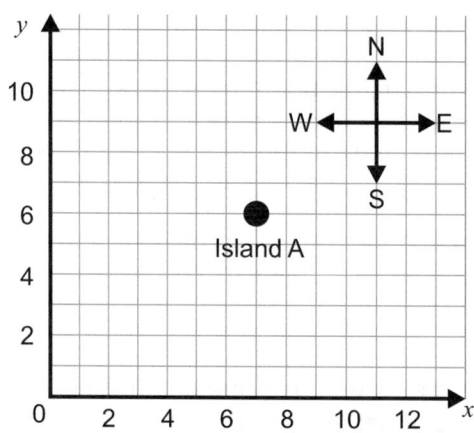

Max wants to row to Island B. Island B is 6 squares west and 5 squares north of Island A. What are the coordinates of Island B?

A (11, 2) **B** (1, 11) **C** (13, 11) **D** (0, 11) **E** (0, 1)

16 Mrs Carraway is a fishmonger. Today, a customer has ordered 3 kg of sardines. Each sardine weighs 80 g. What is the maximum number of sardines that Mrs Carraway can sell to her customer before the total weight exceeds 3 kg?

A 38 **B** 3 **C** 37 **D** 33 **E** 29

17 In the computer game 'Elemental Reckoning', players choose one of the four 'elements', Earth, Fire, Water and Wind, to give them special powers.

Takuma conducts a survey of a sample of 'Elemental Reckoning' players. He asks each player which element is their favourite to use in the game. His findings are shown in the pie chart below.

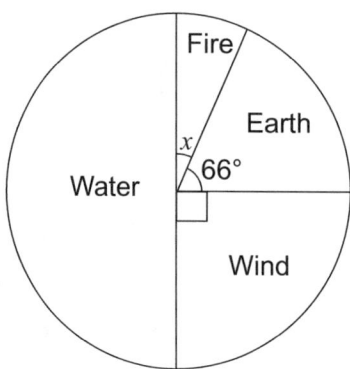

11 players told Takuma that their favourite element was Earth. How many said that their favourite element was Water?

A 60 **B** 30 **C** 66 **D** 22 **E** 33

18 Five people give their ages in a survey. The first four people are 36, 30, 37 and 28. The mean of the five people's ages is 33. How old is the fifth person in the survey?

 A 33 B 34 C 27 D 24 E 31

19 Here is a diagram of a shop's car park.
The car park is made up of a driveway and 10 parking spaces.
Each parking space is the same size.

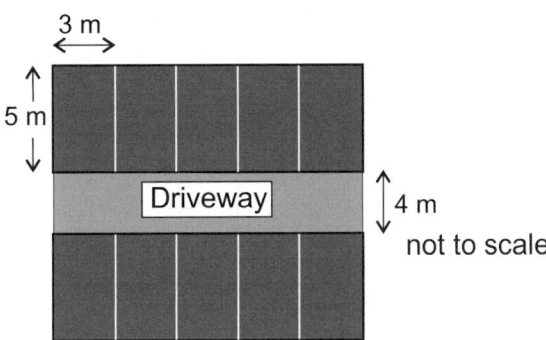

What is the area of the car park?

 A 210 m² B 75 m² C 180 m² D 600 m² E 15 m²

20 Below is a number list. It contains square numbers that are also factors of 72.
The first three numbers in the list are as follows:

1, 4, 9, ...

What is the fourth number in the list?

 A 16 B 24 C 12 D 25 E 36

21 A train contains 8 carriages with 20 seats in each carriage. On a journey to London, the train is so busy that all the seats are full and 12 passengers end up without seats. What is the total number of passengers on the train to London?

 A 80 B 172 C 148 D 232 E 96

22 A runner's score at the end of a race is calculated using these instructions:
Multiply the position the runner came in the race by the course's difficulty rating, then add 10.

A race at Boggy Marsh has a difficulty rating of 2. Which expression gives the score of a runner who raced at Boggy Marsh, where x is the position the runner came in the race?

 A $x + 10 + 2$ B $2x + 10$ C $2x + 10x$ D $10x + 2$ E $10 + x$

23 The graph below shows the temperature in Catherine's garden throughout the day.

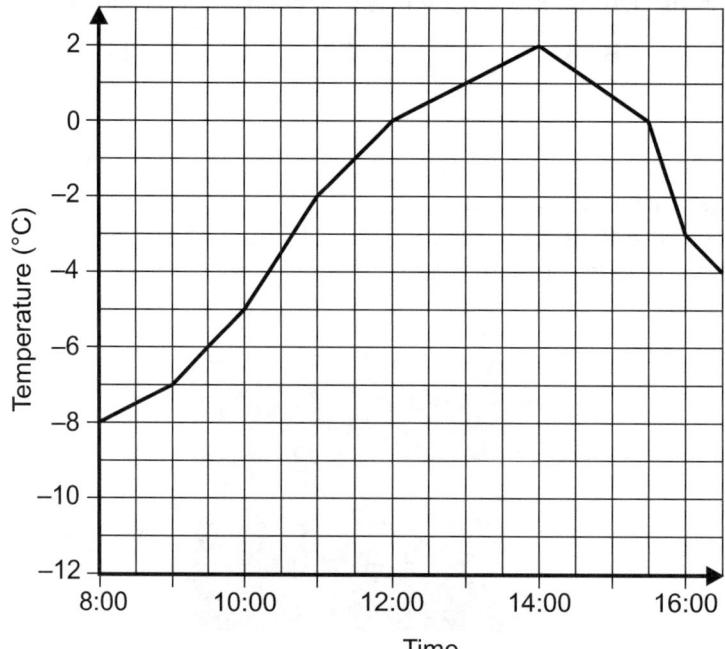

The ice in Catherine's bird bath begins to melt if the temperature rises above 0 °C. For how long in total on the day shown on the graph did this happen?

A 3.25 hours   B 2.75 hours   C 2.5 hours   D 2.25 hours   E 3.5 hours

End of test

CGP

11+ Practice Papers

For the **GL** Buckinghamshire Transfer Test

Answer Book

Ages 10-11

Set A: Paper 1

Section 1: English

Pages 2-10

P1) D
Lines 8-10 state that the tower was built using "4,000 tonnes of steel" and that it is "glazed almost entirely in crystal-clear windows reinforced with silicone and aluminium", showing that steel, glass and aluminium were used in the structure. Line 11 states that there are "concrete foundations". There is no mention of crystal being used to construct the tower.

P2) C
'sucsessful' should be 'successful' — the second 'c' is used for the 's' sound.

P3) A
'in' is correct because it completes the phrase 'to participate in'.

1) C
In the passage, it says that "only a few crumbled ruins remain." There isn't a lot to look at because there isn't much of the castle left.

2) E
In the passage, it says that the castle sits "on a rocky piece of land which juts out into Loch Carron".

3) B
The passage says that the castle "is positioned in a spectacular location."

4) A
In the passage, it says that the castle could "keep a watchful eye on the vessels that went past." The castle's position enabled it to guard the waterway, which is a strategic advantage.

5) A
In the passage, it says that the castle "stood on the border of lands claimed by the two clans". This means that the two clans lived on land next to each other.

6) E
In the passage, it says, "In around 1602, the Mackenzies surrounded the castle, trapping the Macdonalds inside." By stopping the Macdonalds from leaving the castle, the Mackenzies were trying to get them to surrender.

7) B
In the passage, it says that "the Mackenzies surrounded the castle, trapping the Macdonalds inside", and that the women were "nervous under the circumstances". This shows that the women were scared by the attack.

8) A
The Macdonalds' supply of gunpowder was damaged when the women poured water over it, which meant that they couldn't defend themselves.

9) E
In the passage, it says the railings are the only "modern interference". This means that they are the only parts of the ruins which have been added in modern times.

10) C
In this context, "unassuming" means 'modest'.

11) B
In this context, "abruptly" means 'steeply'.

12) B
"berated" means 'scolded'.

13) D
"turbulent" is an adjective as it describes Strome Castle's past.

14) B
"two Macdonald women" is the subject of the sentence because they are doing the action.

15) D
"bore the brunt" means 'received the worst'. The tower was the worst affected by the explosion.

16) B
'ocurs' should be 'occurs' — the word is spelled with a double 'c'.

17) A
'obscureing' should be 'obscuring' — the 'e' is removed when the suffix 'ing' is added.

18) D
'allignment' should be 'alignment' — the word is spelled with one 'l'.

19) B
'fractian' should be 'fraction' — it uses the suffix 'tion'.

20) N
There are no mistakes in this line.

21) D
There shouldn't be a comma between 'door' and 'of' as they are in the same clause.

22) B
The comma should be inside the speech marks.

23) B
There should be a comma between 'driveway' and 'Alice' to separate the adverbial from the rest of the sentence.

24) N
There are no mistakes in this line.

25) C
There should be an apostrophe in 'didnt' because it is the contracted form of 'did not'.

26) C
'onto' is correct — it is the correct preposition for boarding a train.

27) A
'caught' is the correct form of the verb 'to catch' as the rest of the sentence uses the simple past tense.

28) B
'would have' is the correct form of the verb 'would' because it fits with the past tense verb 'ironed'.

29) B
'so' is the adverb that makes the most sense.

30) D
'before' is the preposition that makes the most sense.

Section 2: Verbal Reasoning

Pages 11-16

P1) TS
The first letter in each pair moves forward 4 letters each time. The second letter moves backward 1 letter each time.

P2) director and spectator
The other three perform on a stage.

P3) INK
The complete word is SINKING.

P4) 7
Subtract 3 each time.

P5) enter and prise
'enterprise' is the only correctly spelled word that can be made.

1) LO
The first letter in each pair moves backward 2 letters each time. The second letter moves forward 3 letters each time.

2) JU
The first letter in each pair moves forward 2 letters and then back 1 letter alternately. The second letter moves forward 2 letters each time.

3) CP
The first letter in each pair repeats once, then moves backward 1 letter. The second letter moves forward 1 additional letter each time, i.e. +1, +2, +3, +4, +5.

4) PJ
The first letter in each pair moves backward 2 letters and backward 1 letter alternately. The second letter moves forward 2 letters and then forward 1 letter alternately.

5) ML
The first letter moves backward 3 letters and then forward 1 letter alternately. The second letter moves backward 2 letters each time.

6) minister and knight
The other three are monarchs.

7) analyse and scrutinise
The other three mean 'to keep an eye on'.

8) competent and haughty
The other three mean 'creative'.

9) journey and trip
The other three are things you can travel on.

10) acorn and twig
The other three are types of tree.

11) LIE
The complete word is RELIEVED.

12) RAP
The complete word is SCRAPED.

13) RAT
The complete word is CRATES.

14) EAR
The complete word is SEARCH.

15) ARK
The complete word is MARKING.

16) 20
Subtract 4 each time.

17) 48
Double the number each time.

18) 34
+2, +4, +6, +8, +10

19) 64
The number added halves each time, i.e. +32, +16, +8, +4, +2

20) 5
-5, -7, -9, -11, -13

21) up and roar
'uproar' is the only correctly spelled word that can be made.

22) after and thought
'afterthought' is the only correctly spelled word that can be made.

23) bed and rock
'bedrock' is the only correctly spelled word that can be made.

24) accept and able
'acceptable' is the only correctly spelled word that can be made.

25) heir and loom
'heirloom' is the only correctly spelled word that can be made.

Set A: Paper 2

Section 1: Non-Verbal & Spatial Reasoning

Pages 2-3

P1) D
In all other figures, the hatched shape is in front of the white shape.

P2) C
In all other figures, the two arrows have different arrowheads.

1) D
In all other figures, the arrow is pointing to the circle.

2) E
In all other figures, there is a white square between the black square and the grey square.

3) C
In all other figures, there are two pairs of shapes with different numbers of sides.

4) B
All other figures have a different number of circles on each side of the black stripes.

5) D
All other figures have only two crosses.

6) A
In all other figures, only two types of shading are used.

7) E
In all other figures, the arrow is pointing from a black shape to another black shape.

Pages 4-5

P1) B
Working from top to bottom, the figure is reflected downwards and gets smaller.

P2) D
Working from left to right, the figure rotates 90 degrees clockwise.

8) C
Working from left to right, the star and the inner shape swap shading. The black circle moves from the top left corner to the top right corner.

9) B
Working from left to right, the small shape gains an extra side and moves diagonally across the grid square.

10) C
Working from left to right, the right-hand half of the heart takes on the shading of the square and the square is removed.

11) A
Working from left to right, the small inner shape in each grid square becomes the large outer shape, and the large outer shape becomes the small inner shape. The arrow rotates 45 degrees clockwise and alternates between black and white.

12) E
Working from top to bottom, each figure rotates 45 degrees anticlockwise, including its hatching.

13) B
Each pair of shapes only appears once in each row and column. Each pair of shadings also only appears once in each row and column.

14) D
The shapes in the top two grid squares in each column are combined to make the figure in the bottom grid square of the column. All white shapes become black and all black shapes become white.

Pages 6-7

P1) B
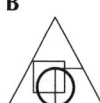

P2) E

15) D
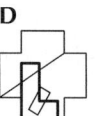

16) B
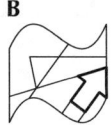

17) B
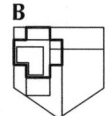

18) E

19) D

20) B

21) D
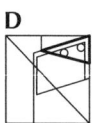

Pages 8-9

P1) B
There are four blocks visible from above, which rules out options A and C. There are two blocks visible on the right-hand side, which rules out options D and E.

P2) C
There are five blocks visible from above, which rules out options A, D and E. There is one block visible at the front, which rules out option B.

22) E
There are five blocks visible from above, which rules out options A, C and D. There is one block visible on the right-hand side, which rules out option B.

23) A
There are five blocks visible from above, which rules out options B, D and E. There are three blocks visible on the right-hand side, which rules out option C.

24) C
There are five blocks visible from above, which rules out option A. There is a row of three blocks at the front of the figure, which rules out options B and D. There are two blocks visible at the back, which rules out option E.

25) B
There are seven blocks visible from above, which rules out options A, C and D. There are two blocks visible at the back, which rules out option E.

26) C
There are six blocks visible from above, which rules out option E. There is one block visible in the second row from the front, which rules out options A, B and D.

27) B
There are six blocks visible from above, which rules out options A and E. There is one block visible at the back, which rules out option C. There are two blocks visible at the front, which rules out option D.

28) D
There are seven blocks visible from above, which rules out options A, B and C. There are three blocks visible on the left-hand side, which rules out option E.

Section 2: Maths
Pages 10-16

P1) £17.94
Round the cost of the football up to £3.00.
£3.00 × 6 = £18.00.
Then take off 6 × £0.01 = £0.06. £18.00 − £0.06 = £17.94.

P2) 20 m
Find 4 on the horizontal axis, which shows the minutes, and then read up to the line. Read across to the vertical axis and you should get 20 metres.

P3) 4
Convert both figures to the same unit of measure.
For example, 3400 g is the same as 3.4 kg.
Work out how many times 3.4 kg goes into 15 kg:
3.4 × 4 = 13.6.
This means there is 15 − 13.6 = 1.4 kg left over.
1.4 kg isn't enough to fill a whole plant pot, so the answer is 4.

1) 50 litres
The tens are the second column to the left of the decimal point. Look at the next column to the right to see whether to round up or down. Here there are 5 ones, so the number rounds up to 50.

2) 21
10% of 140 is 140 ÷ 10 = 14.
5% is half of 10%, so 5% of 140 is 14 ÷ 2 = 7.
So 15% of 140 is 14 + 7 = 21.

3) 43 miles
Work out how many miles Leo has cycled so far:
21 + 52 = 73 and 73 + 34 = 107 miles. Leo wants to cycle 150 miles in total, so he needs to do 150 − 107 = 43 miles.

4) 60.1335
7.245 × 8.3 is the same as 7245 × 83 except there are four digits after the decimal points. Taking 601 335 and moving the decimal point four places to the left gives 60.1335.

5) 8
Reading from the graph, 11 children get to school by car and 3 children get to school by bike.
11 − 3 = 8 more children travel to school by car than by bike.

6) 11 m
11 m is the most likely figure as none of the other options are realistic. 11 cm is about half the width of this page — this is too small. 1.1 km is the length of around 10 football pitches — this would be far too large. 1100 mm = 1.1 m, which is around the height of a wheelie bin — which is too small.

7) 135 cm³
The cuboid's volume is equal to length × width × height, which is 9 × 5 × 3. 9 × 5 = 45 and 45 × 3 = 135.

8) (3, 6)
Count 4 squares to the left of the black cross which marks Joss' house. You need to find the x-coordinate of this point first, then the y-coordinate. Look down from the point you're on and work out the value on the x-axis (3). Then look across from the point you're on and read the value on the y-axis (6).
So the answer is (3, 6).

9) 24
2 lemons make 3.5 glasses, so 2 × 10 = 20 lemons make 3.5 × 10 = 35 glasses.
Another two lemons make 35 + 3.5 = 38.5 glasses, and another two make 38.5 + 3.5 = 42 glasses.
So Anna uses 20 + 2 + 2 = 24 lemons.

10) 24
There are twice as many Golden Retrievers as Collies, so there are 8 ÷ 2 = 4 Collies. Golden Retrievers and Collies together make up half the number of dogs, so the total number of dogs is (8 + 4) × 2 = 12 × 2 = 24.

11) 52°
The angles in a triangle add up to 180°.
Add together the two known angles: 38° + 90° = 128°.
Now subtract this from 180°.
So the missing angle x is 180° − 128° = 52°.

12) 3
If $7a - 2 = 19$, then a number multiplied by 7 gives 2 more than 19, i.e. $7a = 19 + 2 = 21$. The only number that multiplies by 7 to give 21 is 3, so $a = 3$.

13) Tuesday
Rule out the days where it does not look as though half as many parcels as letters were delivered (Monday, Friday and Saturday). Reading the graph for Tuesday, you can see that 15 parcels and 30 letters were delivered.
30 ÷ 15 = 2, so Tuesday is the day when Poe delivered half as many parcels as letters.

14) Prism
A prism is a 3D shape that has the same face at each end. The other shape types do not describe the box.

15) 5
Find 4 on the horizontal axis then read up to the line. Read across to the vertical axis, which tells you that the value is halfway between 4 and 6. So the answer is 5.

16) 130 m
To find the length of the fence, you need to find the outside perimeter of the park. The diagram below shows the lengths you need to add together to calculate the perimeter.

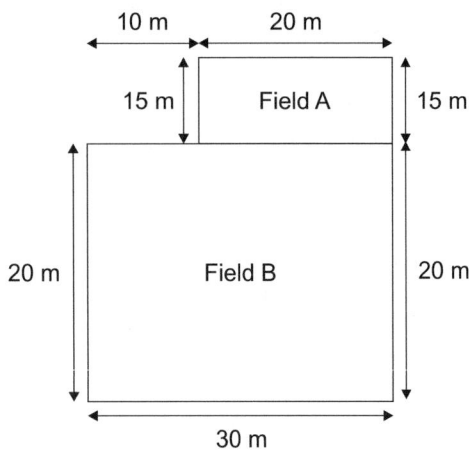

20 + 15 + 20 + 30 + 20 + 10 + 15 = 130 m.

17) 4
Add up all the numbers and divide by the number of days.
5 + 2 + 5 + 1 + 7 + 5 + 3 = 28
28 ÷ 7 days = 4.

18) (2, 14)

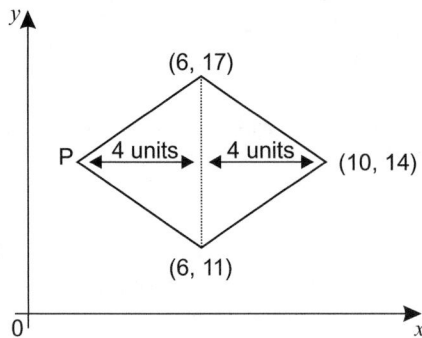

The middle of the rhombus has an x-coordinate of 6 — this is 10 − 6 = 4 places before the x-coordinate of the right hand point. So the x-coordinate of point P will also be 4 places before the x-coordinate of the centre: 6 − 4 = 2. Point P is at the same height as the right hand point so will have the same y-coordinate as the right hand point, which is 14.

19) $\frac{1}{6}$
Lindsey won 5 out of the 30 matches. As a fraction, this is $\frac{5}{30}$. Dividing the numerator and denominator by 5 simplifies this to $\frac{1}{6}$.

20) 0.25
The pictogram shows that Tilda owns 8 Small teapots + 7 Medium teapots + 5 Large teapots = 20 teapots in total. To calculate the proportion of Large teapots, write this as a fraction: $\frac{5}{20}$. Multiplying the numerator and denominator by 5 gives $\frac{25}{100}$. Written as a decimal this is 0.25.

21) $3n + 1$
In each shape, the number of pegs goes up by 3, so the formula must contain $3n$. The 1st shape has 4 pegs, so if $n = 1$, then $3n = 3$, so you need to add 1 to get the correct number of pegs. So the formula is $3n + 1$.

22) 16:03
The train was supposed to set off at 13:30, but it was 20 minutes late, so instead it set off at 13:50. The journey took 2 hours plus a 13-minute delay, so the train arrived in London at 16:03.

23) 53
47 and 45 cannot be in the list because the second digits in these numbers are larger than the first digits. Out of the remaining options only 53 and 61 are prime. 53 is smaller, so it must be the next number the list.

Set B: Paper 1

Section 1: English

Pages 2-9

P1) B
Line 6 states that Dick Turpin "followed in the footsteps of his father to become a butcher", showing that he learnt how to be a butcher from his father.

P2) C
'adressing' should be 'addressing' — the word is spelled with a double 'd'.

P3) C
'from' is the correct preposition to go with the verb 'adapted' in this context.

1) D
In the passage, it says that Tom was "very fond of hunting and tormenting creatures for mere sport."

2) B
Tom has "never seen a caddis with a house-door before". This suggests Tom pulled it open because he was curious.

3) D
In the passage, it says that "her mouth and face were tight tied up in a new night-cap of neat pink skin." This means that her mouth is sealed up.

4) C
The caddises say "there you are at it again" after Tom has broken the door of the caddis' house. "Again" suggests the caddises know that Tom has done things like this before.

5) A
In the passage, it says that Tom feels "as little boys do when they have done wrong and won't say so." Tom knows that he has done something bad, but he hasn't admitted it.

6) E
The creature sheds its exoskeleton and turns into a dragonfly.

7) C
In the passage, the creature says, "I want to be quiet. I want to split." Tom is disturbing the dragonfly's efforts to split.

8) A
The dragonfly isn't unwell. In the passage, it says that the dragonfly is "half ashamed," meaning the dragonfly is self-conscious, so B is true. The passage says the dragonfly is "very pale" when he first splits, so C is true. In the passage, it says that the dragonfly "moved its legs very feebly," meaning the dragonfly finds it difficult to move, so D is true. In the passage, it says that the dragonfly was an "ugly dirty creature" before transforming, but became "slender, elegant, soft", so E is true.

9) E
In the passage the dragonfly says to Tom that "you cannot catch me" and says he is "king of all the flies". This means that he is feeling confident after his transformation.

10) D
"Under" is a preposition, because it describes the position of the creature in relation to the bank.

11) D
'feebly' is an adverb, because it describes a verb — it describes the way the dragonfly moves.

12) C
This is a simile, because the passage says the dragonfly is like a girl.

13) A
"meddlesome" means 'interfering'.

14) C
"slender" means 'lean'.

15) A
"hung" means that the dragonfly was hovering in the air, while "poised" means 'suspended' or 'balanced'.

16) B
'breathe' should be 'breath'. These words are similar, but 'breathe' is a verb and 'breath' is the noun.

17) N
There are no mistakes in this line.

18) D
'asent' should be 'ascent' — it is spelled with a soft 'c'.

19) A
'minature' should be 'miniature' — it is spelled with 'ia'.

20) D
'sumit' should be 'summit' — it is spelled with a double 'm'.

21) C
There should be a colon after 'natural features' instead of a semi-colon, because it is introducing a list.

22) A
There should not be a comma before 'and' because a comma is not needed before the final item in a list.

23) B
'indonesia' should have a capital letter as it is a proper noun.

24) N
There are no mistakes in this line.

25) A
'countries'' shouldn't have an apostrophe, because it isn't showing possession — it's just a plural.

26) A
'for' is correct because it is the correct preposition to go with the verb 'appealing'.

27) C
'who' is the pronoun which makes sense in this sentence.

28) C
'offer' is correct, because it completes the phrase 'on offer'.

29) E
'those' is the pronoun which makes sense in this sentence.

30) B
'for' is the preposition which makes sense in this sentence.

Section 2: Verbal Reasoning

Pages 10-16

P1) frail and hearty
'frail' means 'in poor health', whereas 'hearty' means 'healthy'.

P2) 3142
S = 3, T = 1, A = 4, R = 2

P3) Dan
Dan only found one egg. Maisie and Aminah found three eggs, and Charlotte and Tony found two eggs.

P4) r
The new words are 'dawn' and 'trip'.

P5) B
9 − 3 = 6, B = 6

P6) p
The new words are 'steep', 'peel', 'shop' and 'park'.

1) overbearing and meek
'overbearing' means 'bossy', whereas 'meek' means 'submissive'.

2) rude and courteous
'rude' means 'impolite', whereas 'courteous' means 'polite'.

3) unity and division
'unity' means 'being together', whereas 'division' means 'being separated'.

4) arrest and liberate
'arrest' means 'to take into custody', whereas 'liberate' means 'to set free'.

5) reward and penalise
'reward' means 'to honour', whereas 'penalise' means 'to punish'.

6) 2316
C = 2, R = 3, A = 1, B = 6

7) 6514
B = 6, E = 5, A = 1, M = 4

8) MARE
M = 4, A = 1, R = 3, E = 5

9) Andrew
Andrew has four scoops of ice cream — vanilla, raspberry, strawberry and chocolate. This is more than anyone else.

10) Tuesday
Tuesday has the smallest number of trains because it has fewer trains than Monday, and Monday has fewer trains than Thursday and Friday. Wednesday has the largest number of trains.

11) s
The new words are 'coat' and 'hiss'.

12) r
The new words are 'shot' and 'free'.

13) n
The new words are 'rage' and 'went'.

14) e
The new words are 'blow' and 'code'.

15) t
The new words are 'sage' and 'seat'.

16) B
9 − 5 = 4, B = 4

17) C
2 + 5 − 3 = 4, C = 4

18) E
8 ÷ 2 + 6 = 10, E = 10

19) B
3 × 4 − 8 = 4, B = 4

20) D
12 ÷ 4 × 3 = 9, D = 9

21) g
The new words are 'king', 'grow', 'song' and 'gate'.

22) p
The new words are 'warp', 'pact', 'ramp' and 'page'.

23) h
The new words are 'gash', 'heel', 'with' and 'hand'.

24) f
The new words are 'beef', 'four', 'scarf' and 'fail'.

25) d
The new words are 'plead', 'down', 'seed' and 'dash'.

Set B: Paper 2

Section 1: Non-Verbal & Spatial Reasoning

Pages 2-3

P1) E
In all figures, there must be one black triangle, one grey triangle and one white triangle.

P2) D
In all figures, there must be two shapes that are identical apart from rotation.

1) C
In all figures, there must be two shapes that are identical apart from shading. One must be above the other, and they must be touching. There must be two smaller versions of the same shape in the centre of each shape. These must have the opposite shading to the larger shapes.

2) D
All figures must only contain lines in parallel pairs.

3) E
In all figures, there must be two fewer lines than the shape has sides.

4) C
In all figures, there must be a dashed line overlapping a shape. Two circles must be on the same side of the line.

5) B
All figures must contain eight squares. The arrow points through a line of symmetry.

6) E
In all figures, all hatched shapes must be in front of the white shape. Two shapes must have their hatching pointing in the same direction and the hatching of the third shape must be in a different direction.

7) D
In all figures, a shape is reflected and there is a small gap between the two shapes. The number of circles in this gap is the same as the number of sides of the shape.

Pages 4-5

P1) C
The code is NY.
M = grey triangles, N = black triangles.
X = three triangles, Y = two triangles.

P2) E
The code is LK.
L = dashed line, M = solid line, N = dotted line.
J = square arrowheads, K = triangle arrowheads.

8) A
The code is GP.
F = vertical line, G = horizontal line, H = diagonal line.
P = black circle, Q = grey circle.

9) B
The code is TZ.
T = three circles, U = four circles, V = two circles.
Y = spiral goes anticlockwise from centre, Z = spiral goes clockwise from centre.

10) A
The code is N.
M = shape has one curved side, N = shape has two curved sides.

11) C
The code is UR.
T = the squares have different orientations,
U = the squares have the same orientation.
P = the arrow points upwards
Q = the arrow points diagonally down to the right,
R = the arrow points diagonally up to the right.

12) B
The code is XNT.
W = grey triangle, X = black triangle, Y = white triangle.
M = arrow points left, N = arrow points right.
S = half of rectangle closest to triangle is black,
T = half of rectangle closest to triangle is white.

13) A
The code is QLF.
P = four-pointed star, Q = six-pointed star, R = five-pointed star.
L = star is on the left, M = star is on the right,
N = star is in the middle.
F = five-sided shape, G = four-sided shape.

14) E
The code is GS.
F = the second rectangle is white,
G = the second rectangle is hatched,
H = the second rectangle is grey.
R = the hatching goes diagonally upwards from right to left,
S = the hatching goes diagonally upwards from left to right.

Pages 6-7

P1) F
Shape F has been rotated 90 degrees left-to-right.

P2) C
Shape C has been rotated 180 degrees in the plane of the page.

15) D
Shape D has been rotated 90 degrees towards you, top-to-bottom.

16) F
Shape F has been rotated 90 degrees right-to-left. It has then been rotated 90 degrees clockwise in the plane of the page.

17) A
Shape A has been rotated 90 degrees left-to-right.

18) C
Shape C has been rotated 90 degrees away from you, top-to-bottom. It has then been rotated 180 degrees in the plane of the page.

19) E
Shape E has been rotated 90 degrees, right-to-left.

20) B
Shape B has been rotated 90 degrees anticlockwise in the plane of the page. It has then been rotated 90 degrees, right-to-left.

Pages 8-9

P1) B
Option A is ruled out because the grey diamond and the black stripe must be on opposite sides. Option C is ruled out because there is no white star on the net. Option D is ruled out because the black star and the white hexagon must be on opposite sides. Option E is ruled out because there is no black circle on the net.

P2) B
Option A is ruled out because there is no grey triangle on the net. Option C is ruled out because the two circles and the oval must be on opposite sides. Option D is ruled out because if the heart was on the top and the triangle was at the front, the two circles would be on the right. Option E is ruled out because the white triangle and the white pentagon must be on opposite sides.

21) D
Option A is ruled out because there is only one white circle on the net. Option B is ruled out because the grey arrow and the grey stripes must be on opposite sides. Option C is ruled out because the black face and the black diagonal stripe must be on opposite sides. Option E is ruled out because the black star and the white circle must be on opposite sides.

22) A
Option B is ruled out because if the black stripe was on the top and the triangle was at the front, the black circle would be on the right. Option C is ruled out because there is no white rectangle on the net. Option D is ruled out because the white circle and the black circle must be on opposite sides. Option E is ruled out because the white triangle and the grey rectangle must be on opposite sides.

23) C
Option A is ruled out because the 'H' shape and the grey face must be on opposite sides. Option B is ruled out because the white trapezium and the grey hexagon must be on opposite sides. Option D is ruled out because the white face and the black circle must be on opposite sides. Option E is ruled out because there is no white hexagon on the net.

24) B
Option A is ruled out because the black square and the letter 'Y' must be on opposite sides. Option C is ruled out because there is only one grey triangle on the net. Option D is ruled out because the letter 'Y' has the wrong rotation. Option E is ruled out because there is only one black square on the net.

25) E
Option A is ruled out because if the white face was on the top and the grey face was at the front, the arrow shape would be on the right. Option B is ruled out because there is only one black rectangle on the net. Option C is ruled out because the white face and the black rectangle must be on opposite sides. Option D is ruled out because the grey face and the black cross shape must be on opposite sides.

26) D
Option A is ruled out because the black circle and the three diagonal lines must be on opposite sides. Option B is ruled out because if the star was on the top and the circle was at the front, the black stripe would be on the right. Option C is ruled out because the black stripe has the wrong rotation. Option E is ruled out because the grey pentagon and the black stripe must be on opposite sides.

27) E
Option A is ruled out because the white circle and the black L-shape must be on opposite sides. Option B is ruled out because there is no white arrow on the net. Option C is ruled out because one of the arrowheads should be pointing at the black L-shape. Option D is ruled out because the white L-shape has been rotated.

Section 2: Maths
Pages 10-16

P1) 53
You need to work out 212 ÷ 4.
You can do this using partitioning.
212 splits into 200 + 12.
200 ÷ 4 = 50 and 12 ÷ 4 = 3.
So 212 ÷ 4 is 50 + 3 = 53.

P2) 48 cm^3
The volume of a cuboid is equal to length × width × height.
So 2 × 3 = 6, 6 × 8 = 48 cm^3.

P3) 1 litre
1 litre is the most likely figure as none of the other options are realistic. 1 millilitre is too small, as is 10 millilitres. 0.01 litres is the same as 10 millilitres so it is also too small. 100 litres is too large.

1) 15°
Angles in a triangle add up to 180°.
Add together the two known angles: 75° + 90° = 165°.
Now subtract this from 180°: angle x = 180° − 165° = 15°.

2) 58 000
The thousands are the fourth column from the right. Look at the column to the right of the thousands to see whether to round up or down. Here there are 6 hundreds, so the number rounds up to 58 000.

3) ¾
Write each fraction as a percentage and see which is closest to 71%. ½ is the same as 50%. ⅘ is the same as 80%. ¼ is the same as 25%. ¾ is the same as 75%. ⁶⁄₁₀ is the same as 60%.
75% is the closest to 71%, so the answer is ¾.

4) 27
Work backwards to reverse the operations.
14 − 5 = 9, and 9 × 3 = 27.
So Amrita's original number was 27.

5) 10.5 km
4500 m is the same as 4.5 km, so the distance between the bank and the restaurant is 15 − 4.5 = 10.5 km.

6) 3 km
The length of the track is 500 m + 500 m + 250 m + 250 m = 1500 m. Blair does 2 laps around the track, so the total distance she travels is 1500 m × 2 = 3000 m, which is the same as 3 km.

7) 732.8
458 × 1.6 is the same as 458 × 0.16 except there is only one digit after the decimal point. Taking 73.28 and moving the decimal point one place to the right gives 732.8.

8) 4
You are told that Abbey won 9 races. If Abbey won 3 more races than Candy, this means that Candy won 9 − 3 = 6 races. If Candy won 6 times as many races as Buddy, this means that Buddy won 6 ÷ 6 = 1 race. To find the number of races that Derek won, you need to add the number of races that everybody else won and subtract this from the total number of races completed.
9 + 6 + 1 = 16. 20 − 16 = 4.

9) Remy
The smallest difference between longest and shortest jumps is shown by the line on the graph where the circle and the cross are closest together. (Remy's longest jump was 10 m and his shortest jump was 9 m. The difference between the two is 10 − 9 = 1 m, the smallest difference of any of the students.)

10) 14:52
First, work out how many lots of 4 km there are in 32 km:
32 ÷ 4 = 8.
Then multiply the time it took Alfred to travel 4 km by this number.
14 × 8 = 112. This is 1 hour and 52 minutes.
1 hour and 52 minutes after 13:00 is 14:52.

11) 54 m
You are told that Apriya starts the race 5 metres ahead of Ben.
So after one lap, he is 5 × 2 = 10, 10 + 2 = 12 m ahead of Ben.
After 2 laps, he is 12 × 2 = 24, 24 + 2 = 26 m ahead of Ben.
After 3 laps, he is 26 × 2 = 52, 52 + 2 = 54 m ahead of Ben.

12) $\frac{1}{5}$
The shape that Raheem has shaded can be found by counting squares: 15 full squares and 10 half squares, which in total is 20 full squares. The piece of paper has 100 squares so the fraction of paper that is shaded is $\frac{20}{100}$. Dividing the numerator and denominator by 20 simplifies this to $\frac{1}{5}$.

13) Lemon
The amount the bakery made of each cake is shown by the overall height of each bar on the graph. Listing the cakes in order from the most to the least made is: Carrot, Chocolate, Lemon, Coffee, Walnut. So the one in the middle is Lemon.

14) 52
The 10th number can be found by substituting n = 10 into the equation: (5 × 10) + 2 = 52.

15) (1, 11)
Island A has coordinates of (7, 6).
Moving 6 squares west will take Max to (1, 6).
Moving 5 squares north will take Max to (1, 11).

16) 37
3 kg is the same as 3000 g. Work out how many lots of 80 are in 3000. The weight of 10 sardines is 80 × 10 = 800 g.
So the weight of 30 sardines is 3 × 800 = 2400 g.
3000 − 2400 = 600 g, so there are 600 g more of sardines needed to reach 3000 g. In 600 g, there are 600 ÷ 80 = 7.5 sardines. So the biggest whole number of sardines in 600 g is 7, meaning there are 37 sardines.

17) 30
11 players chose Earth.
The angle of the Earth sector on the pie chart is 66°, so 66° is the same as 11 players. So one person is represented by 66° ÷ 11 = 6°. The Water sector has an angle of 180°, so the number of players who chose Water = 180° ÷ 6° = 30.

18) 34
The mean of the 5 ages is 33.
So the sum of the 5 ages is 5 × 33 = 165.
The four ages that you know add up to:
36 + 30 + 37 + 28 = 131.
So the fifth person is 165 − 131 = 34 years old.

19) 210 m²
The total length of the car park = 5 m + 4 m + 5 m = 14 m.
The total width of the car park = 3 m × 5 = 15 m.
So the area of the car park = 15 × 14 = (10 × 14) + (5 × 14)
= 140 + 70 = 210 m².

20) 36
The next square number after 9 is 4 × 4 = 16, but 16 isn't a factor of 72. 5 × 5 = 25 is the next square number, but 25 isn't a factor of 72. The next square number is 6 × 6 = 36 and 72 ÷ 2 = 36, so the next number in the list is 36.

21) 172
All the seats are full, so the number of passengers with seats is 20 × 8 = 160. The number of passengers without seats is 12, so the total number of passengers on the train is 160 + 12 = 172.

22) $2x + 10$
The runner's position in the race is x and Boggy Marsh's difficulty rating is 2, so the expression must be related to $2x$. Then add 10 points on, so the correct expression is $2x + 10$.

23) 3.5 hours
Find the two points on the graph where the temperature was 0 °C: these are at 12:00 and 15:30. The length of time that it was above 0 °C is the difference between these two times: 15:30 is 3 hours and 30 minutes after 12:00. This is the same as 3.5 hours.

CGP

11+ Practice Papers

For the **GL** Buckinghamshire Transfer Test

Answer Sheets

Ages 10-11

Using the Multiple Choice Answer Sheets

Multiple Choice papers are often marked by a computer.
These papers use special answer sheets like the ones in this booklet.

There's a Multiple Choice answer sheet to go with each Practice Paper, so make sure you're filling in the right one. If you get used to these answer sheets now, it means there'll be no nasty surprises when you sit the real test.

Here are a few tips for using the answer sheets without getting yourself in a pickle...

Tips for Filling in the Answer Sheets

1) Before you start, fill in your name and the name of your school in the correct space. There may be boxes for other information, like your date of birth or your candidate number. Make sure you don't leave anything blank by mistake.

2) To mark your answer, put a clear pencil line in the answer box.

3) Make sure you have a pencil sharpener and an eraser for any mistakes.

4) If you make a mistake, rub out the incorrect answer first, and then fill in your new answer clearly.

5) It's easy to lose your place when you move from the test paper to the answer sheet, so match up the question number on the paper and the answer sheet. Keeping the two sheets close together will help you do this.

6) If you skip a question to come back to later, make sure you leave a gap for that question on the answer sheet. That way your answers will stay in order.

7) Don't do rough working on your answer sheet.

8) Don't worry if you mark boxes in the same position several times in a row — just because you've marked the second box four times, it doesn't mean that your answers are wrong.

Practice Paper — Set A: Paper 1

CGP

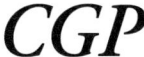

Candidate's name:

School name:

Date of Test		
Day	Month	Year

Date of Birth		
Day	Month	Year

Candidate Number

School Number

Please mark like this: ▭

A1

EXAMPLE: A (marked) B C D E

P1: A B C D E

EXAMPLE: A B C (marked) D N

P2: A B C D N

EXAMPLE: A B C D (marked) E

P3: A B C D E

1: A B C D E

2: A B C D E

3: A B C D E

4: A B C D E

5: A B C D E

6: A B C D E

7: A B C D E

8: A B C D E

9: A B C D E

10: A B C D E

11: A B C D E

12: A B C D E

13: A B C D E

14: A B C D E

15: A B C D E

16: A B C D N

17: A B C D N

18: A B C D N

19: A B C D N

20: A B C D N

21: A B C D N

22: A B C D N

23: A B C D N

24: A B C D N

25: A B C D N

26: A B C D E

27: A B C D E

28: A B C D E

29: A B C D E

30: A B C D E

 © CGP 2019

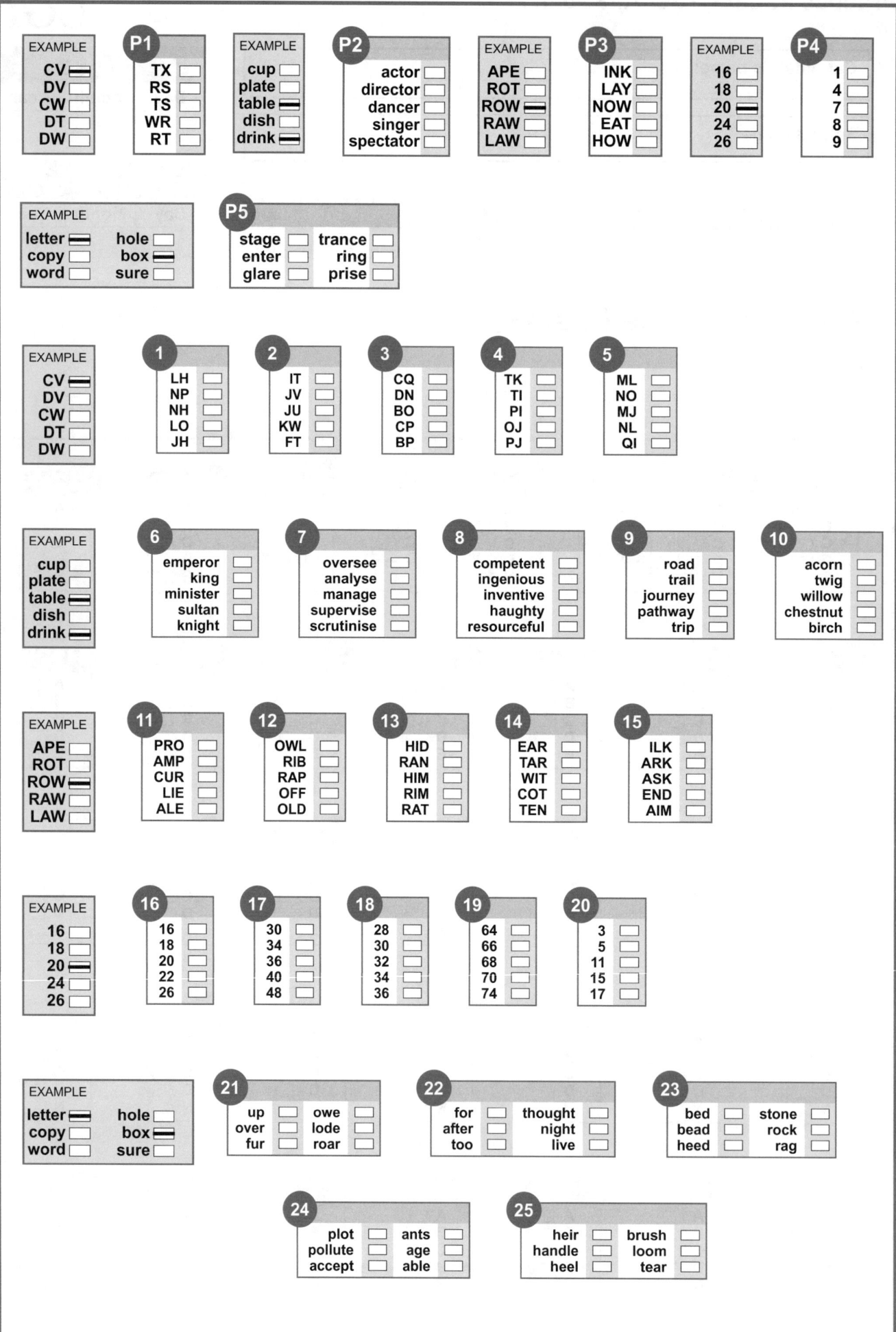

Practice Paper — Set A: Paper 2

CGP

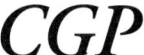

Candidate's name:

School name:

Date of Test		
Day	Month	Year

Date of Birth		
Day	Month	Year

Candidate Number

School Number

Please mark like this:

A2

EXAMPLE: a b c d e
P1: a b c d e
P2: a b c d e
1: a b c d e
2: a b c d e
3: a b c d e
4: a b c d e
5: a b c d e
6: a b c d e

7: a b c d e
EXAMPLE: a b c d e
P1: a b c d e
P2: a b c d e
8: a b c d e
9: a b c d e
10: a b c d e
11: a b c d e

12: a b c d e
13: a b c d e
14: a b c d e
EXAMPLE: a b c d e
P1: a b c d e
P2: a b c d e
15: a b c d e
16: a b c d e

17: a b c d e
18: a b c d e
19: a b c d e
20: a b c d e
21: a b c d e
EXAMPLE: a b c d e
P1: a b c d e
P2: a b c d e

22: a b c d e
23: a b c d e
24: a b c d e
25: a b c d e
26: a b c d e
27: a b c d e
28: a b c d e

© CGP 2019

EXAMPLE	P1	P2	P3	1	2	3
3/4 ▬	£17.94 ☐	30 m ☐	14 ☐	50 litres ☐	14 ☐	53 miles ☐
1/2 ☐	£18.00 ☐	20 m ☐	2 ☐	45 litres ☐	70 ☐	47 miles ☐
10/16 ☐	£6.00 ☐	10 m ☐	8 ☐	40 litres ☐	20 ☐	23 miles ☐
18/36 ☐	£19.74 ☐	0 m ☐	4 ☐	46 litres ☐	27 ☐	43 miles ☐
1/5 ☐	£18.64 ☐	5 m ☐	6 ☐	60 litres ☐	21 ☐	97 miles ☐

4	5	6	7	8	9	10
6013.35 ☐	11 ☐	11 m ☐	76 cm³ ☐	(6, 11) ☐	22 ☐	24 ☐
60.1335 ☐	2 ☐	11 cm ☐	180 cm³ ☐	(4, 6) ☐	24 ☐	12 ☐
6.01335 ☐	7 ☐	1.1 km ☐	48 cm³ ☐	(11, 6) ☐	26 ☐	4 ☐
601.335 ☐	8 ☐	1100 mm ☐	17 cm³ ☐	(3, 6) ☐	28 ☐	16 ☐
0.601335 ☐	6 ☐	1.1 m ☐	135 cm³ ☐	(7, 4) ☐	32 ☐	36 ☐

11	12	13	14	15	16	17
42° ☐	2 ☐	Monday ☐	Prism ☐	6 ☐	900 m ☐	5 ☐
38° ☐	3 ☐	Tuesday ☐	Cube ☐	4 ☐	150 m ☐	3 ☐
58° ☐	4 ☐	Wednesday ☐	Rectangle ☐	3 ☐	130 m ☐	7 ☐
90° ☐	5 ☐	Thursday ☐	Pyramid ☐	7 ☐	85 m ☐	4 ☐
52° ☐	6 ☐	Friday ☐	Trapezium ☐	5 ☐	100 m ☐	9 ☐

18	19	20	21	22	23
(10, 6) ☐	1/6 ☐	0.8 ☐	$3n + 3$ ☐	16:03 ☐	47 ☐
(4, 14) ☐	5/24 ☐	0.125 ☐	$3n + 1$ ☐	15:37 ☐	61 ☐
(2, 14) ☐	1/2 ☐	0.25 ☐	$n + 4$ ☐	15:03 ☐	51 ☐
(14, 10) ☐	5/19 ☐	0.5 ☐	$4n + 3$ ☐	15:23 ☐	53 ☐
(2, 17) ☐	1/4 ☐	0.4 ☐	$3n + 4$ ☐	16:23 ☐	45 ☐

Practice Paper — Set B: Paper 1

Candidate's name:

School name:

Date of Test		
Day	Month	Year

Candidate Number

School Number

Date of Birth		
Day	Month	Year

Please mark like this: ⊟

B1

Answer Sheet

EXAMPLE: good ▬, tasty ☐, sweet ☐, dark ☐, dirty ☐, bad ▬

P1: vulnerable ☐, frail ☐, puny ☐, hearty ☐, gleeful ☐, capable ☐

EXAMPLE: 2413 ▬, 1463 ☐, 6352 ☐, 2143 ☐, 6335 ☐

P2: 7234 ☐, 3841 ☐, 6841 ☐, 3142 ☐, 7431 ☐

EXAMPLE: Kemal ☐, Maya ▬, Luke ☐, Erica ☐, Sajid ☐

P3: Maisie ☐, Aminah ☐, Tony ☐, Charlotte ☐, Dan ☐

EXAMPLE: p ▬, e ☐, a ☐, c ☐, h ☐

P4: d ☐, r ☐, a ☐, w ☐, n ☐

EXAMPLE: A ☐, B ☐, C ☐, D ▬, E ☐

P5: A ☐, B ☐, C ☐, D ☐, E ☐

EXAMPLE: a ☐, e ▬, d ☐, k ☐, g ☐

P6: t ☐, p ☐, r ☐, d ☐, l ☐

EXAMPLE: good ▬, tasty ☐, sweet ☐, dark ☐, dirty ☐, bad ▬

1: overbearing ☐, reckless ☐, calm ☐, reasonable ☐, polite ☐, meek ☐

2: rude ☐, tender ☐, naive ☐, courteous ☐, ignorant ☐, obliging ☐

3: exchange ☐, collection ☐, unity ☐, dissection ☐, division ☐, displacement ☐

4: stop ☐, arrest ☐, punish ☐, liberate ☐, extract ☐, disentangle ☐

5: recommend ☐, provide ☐, reward ☐, criticise ☐, penalise ☐, argue ☐

6: 7145 ☐, 3135 ☐, 2316 ☐, 6513 ☐, 2135 ☐

7: 6132 ☐, 3415 ☐, 2453 ☐, 1273 ☐, 6514 ☐

8: MANE ☐, MARE ☐, RACE ☐, AREA ☐, CRAM ☐

9: Diana ☐, Alastair ☐, Rachel ☐, Jenny ☐, Andrew ☐

10: Monday ☐, Tuesday ☐, Wednesday ☐, Thursday ☐, Friday ☐

EXAMPLE: p ▬, e ☐, a ☐, c ☐, h ☐

11: c ☐, o ☐, a ☐, s ☐, t ☐

12: s ☐, h ☐, o ☐, r ☐, t ☐

13: r ☐, a ☐, n ☐, g ☐, e ☐

14: b ☐, e ☐, l ☐, o ☐, w ☐

15: s ☐, t ☐, a ☐, g ☐, e ☐

EXAMPLE: A ☐, B ☐, C ☐, D ▬, E ☐

16: A ☐, B ☐, C ☐, D ☐, E ☐

17: A ☐, B ☐, C ☐, D ☐, E ☐

18: A ☐, B ☐, C ☐, D ☐, E ☐

19: A ☐, B ☐, C ☐, D ☐, E ☐

20: A ☐, B ☐, C ☐, D ☐, E ☐

EXAMPLE: a ☐, e ▬, d ☐, k ☐, g ☐

21: d ☐, g ☐, c ☐, p ☐, s ☐

22: m ☐, f ☐, p ☐, d ☐, e ☐

23: p ☐, f ☐, s ☐, l ☐, h ☐

24: m ☐, n ☐, r ☐, f ☐, d ☐

25: d ☐, n ☐, t ☐, k ☐, p ☐

11+ / GL / Buckinghamshire / Answer Sheets

Practice Paper — Set B: Paper 2

CGP

Candidate's name:

School name:

Date of Test		
Day	Month	Year

Date of Birth		
Day	Month	Year

Candidate Number

School Number

Please mark like this:

B2

EXAMPLE: a b c d e
P1: a b c d e
P2: a b c d e
1: a b c d e
2: a b c d e
3: a b c d e
4: a b c d e
5: a b c d e
6: a b c d e
7: a b c d e

EXAMPLE: a b c d e
P1: a b c d e
P2: a b c d e
8: a b c d e
9: a b c d e
10: a b c d e
11: a b c d e
12: a b c d e
13: a b c d e
14: a b c d e

EXAMPLE: a b
P1: a b c d e f
P2: a b c d e f
15: a b c d e f
16: a b c d e f
17: a b c d e f
18: a b c d e f
19: a b c d e f
20: a b c d e f

EXAMPLE: a b c d e
P1: a b c d e
P2: a b c d e
21: a b c d e
22: a b c d e
23: a b c d e
24: a b c d e
25: a b c d e
26: a b c d e
27: a b c d e

© CGP 2019

EXAMPLE	P1	P2	P3	1	2	3
£7.75 ▬	43 ☐	64 cm³ ☐	1 millilitre ☐	75° ☐	58 000 ☐	½ ☐
£6.23 ☐	52 ☐	44 millilitres ☐	10 millilitres ☐	165° ☐	57 000 ☐	⁴/₅ ☐
£7.76 ☐	53 ☐	26 cm³ ☐	1 litre ☐	25° ☐	59 000 ☐	¾ ☐
£8.99 ☐	63 ☐	48 cm³ ☐	100 litres ☐	105° ☐	57 500 ☐	¼ ☐
£8.76 ☐	64 ☐	32 cm³ ☐	0.01 litres ☐	15° ☐	60 000 ☐	⁶/₁₀ ☐

4	5	6	7	8	9	10
57 ☐	11 500 m ☐	1.5 km ☐	7.328 ☐	6 ☐	Claire ☐	15:08 ☐
27 ☐	30 km ☐	2.5 km ☐	7328 ☐	3 ☐	Bill ☐	14:38 ☐
55 ☐	9 km ☐	0.75 km ☐	732.8 ☐	5 ☐	Jason ☐	13:56 ☐
3 ☐	4500 m ☐	3 km ☐	7.238 ☐	4 ☐	Remy ☐	15:12 ☐
29 ☐	10.5 km ☐	1.25 km ☐	0.7328 ☐	7 ☐	Tiffany ☐	14:52 ☐

11	12	13	14	15	16	17
54 m ☐	⅕ ☐	Walnut ☐	70 ☐	(11, 2) ☐	38 ☐	60 ☐
12 m ☐	³/₁₀ ☐	Carrot ☐	10 ☐	(1, 11) ☐	3 ☐	30 ☐
30 m ☐	½ ☐	Lemon ☐	52 ☐	(13, 11) ☐	37 ☐	66 ☐
62 m ☐	⁸/₁₀ ☐	Chocolate ☐	17 ☐	(0, 11) ☐	33 ☐	22 ☐
64 m ☐	⅖ ☐	Coffee ☐	47 ☐	(0, 1) ☐	29 ☐	33 ☐

18	19	20	21	22	23
33 ☐	210 m² ☐	16 ☐	80 ☐	$x + 10 + 2$ ☐	3.25 hours ☐
34 ☐	75 m² ☐	24 ☐	172 ☐	$2x + 10$ ☐	2.75 hours ☐
27 ☐	180 m² ☐	12 ☐	148 ☐	$2x + 10x$ ☐	2.5 hours ☐
24 ☐	600 m² ☐	25 ☐	232 ☐	$10x + 2$ ☐	2.25 hours ☐
31 ☐	15 m² ☐	36 ☐	96 ☐	$10 + x$ ☐	3.5 hours ☐

BLANK PAGE

CGP

11+ Practice Papers

For the **GL** Buckinghamshire Transfer Test

Parents' Guide

Ages 10-11

Published by CGP

Editors:
Eleanor Claringbold, Emma Clayton, Georgina Fairclough, Katie Fernandez, Paul Jordin, Luke Molloy and Matt Topping

Many thanks to Emma Cleasby, Sharon Keeley-Holden and Hayley Thompson for the proofreading.

Please note that CGP is not associated with GL Assessment in any way. These tests do not include any official questions and are not endorsed by GL Assessment.

ISBN: 978 1 78908 448 1

Printed by Elanders Ltd, Newcastle upon Tyne.
Clipart from Corel®

Text, design, layout and original illustrations
© Coordination Group Publications Ltd. (CGP) 2019
All rights reserved.

Photocopying more than 5% of a paper is not permitted, even if you have a CLA licence.
Extra copies are available from CGP with next day delivery • 0800 1712 712 • www.cgpbooks.co.uk

What This Pack Contains

What this pack contains

This pack contains **two sets** of 11+ Practice Papers for the Buckinghamshire Secondary Transfer Test set by GL.

The questions in these papers have been written to match the level of difficulty of the real exam. They are designed to test your child's English, Verbal Reasoning, Maths, Non-Verbal and Spatial Reasoning skills.

Each of the practice papers in this pack has an accompanying **multiple-choice answer sheet**, just like the answer sheets used in the real 11+ exams. There are also **full answers** to every question in the separate **answer booklet**.

You can also download and play the **online audio instructions**, which are similar to the instructions that your child will hear on test day. (Depending on the format of the test in your area, the instructions could be played as an audio recording, like the ones we have provided, or they may be read aloud by an exam invigilator.)

You can find the audio downloads at:

cgpbooks.co.uk/11plustestaudio

This set of papers also includes a **free Online Edition**. For details of how to access your Online Edition, just follow the instructions in the box below:

How to access your free Online Edition

This book includes a free Online Edition to read on your PC, Mac or tablet.
You'll just need to go to **cgpbooks.co.uk/extras** and enter this code:

4279 9725 6186 7895

By the way, this code only works for one person. If somebody else has used this book before you, they might have already claimed the Online Edition.

The pages that follow in this Parents' Guide are designed to give some guidance and information on how to best prepare for the 11+ test, as well as how to support your child in performing as well as they can.

- It's important to remember that preparing to take the 11+ can be a stressful time for both parents and pupils. You should do all you can to minimise pressure for the whole family, and try to make the whole process as positive an experience as possible.
- When studying for the 11+, your child will learn plenty of new skills that can have a beneficial impact on their whole education, regardless of whether they pass the 11+ test.
- With the right mindset and preparation, your child will be able to approach the test with confidence, and come out of it feeling positive about their performance.

What is the 11+?

It can be tricky to find reliable information about the 11+ and how to prepare for it. This page covers the basics — what the 11+ test is and how it works.

The 11+ is a selective test

Most secondary schools in the UK are comprehensive — they're non-selective and accept children of all abilities. But in some areas, selective state secondary schools (grammar schools) still exist. These schools select their pupils based on academic ability.

The 11+ test is used to determine if a child is suitable for grammar school. It's also used for entry to some independent schools. Children usually sit the test in the first term of their last year at primary school.

Some schools select pupils based just on the 11+ test results, but others look at other factors, e.g. whether you live close to the school, or if you have other children at the school.

The format of the test varies

The exact format of the 11+ test varies depending on the school or Local Authority (LA) you're applying to, as well as on the provider that sets the test. There are two main providers for the 11+ — **GL Assessment** and **CEM**. However, in some cases, the test papers will be written by the school, or by a consortium of schools in that area. The format of the Buckinghamshire Test is described at the bottom of this page.

Wherever you are, there are four main subjects that can be tested:

> **Verbal Reasoning** — problem-solving and logic using words, letters, numbers, etc.
> **Non-Verbal Reasoning** — problem-solving and logic using pictures and symbols.
> **Maths** — often at the same level as the SATs, but it may be more challenging.
> **English** — reading comprehension, grammar and sometimes a writing task.

Tests set by GL Assessment can include any combination of these four subjects (you won't necessarily have to do all four). Traditionally, there would be a different test paper for each subject — however, some GL regions now have mixed papers, with two papers that each cover more than one subject.

Papers set by CEM are usually mixed, and will cover Verbal Reasoning, Non-Verbal Reasoning and Maths. However, CEM Verbal Reasoning does contain some of the same elements as GL English, such as comprehension.

The tests are usually either **multiple choice** (MC) or **standard answer** (SA) format.

> **Multiple choice** — there's a separate answer sheet. There's usually a choice of five options for each answer, and the answers may be computer-marked.
> **Standard answer** — there are spaces on the question paper for the pupil to write their own answers. There will usually not be any answer options given for the pupil to choose from.

The Buckinghamshire Test

The Buckinghamshire Test is set by GL Assessment, and Buckinghamshire is one of the GL areas that has **mixed papers**:

> One paper tests **English** and **Verbal Reasoning** skills.
> The other paper tests **Maths** and **Non-Verbal** and **Spatial Reasoning** skills.

The front covers of the practice papers in this pack give more information on the structure and timings of the test. The Buckinghamshire Test is a **multiple-choice** test.

Using the Practice Papers

This advice will help you to get the most out of this set of practice papers. You may wish to administer the practice papers in exam conditions to help your child become familiar with the format of the test.

These practice papers are in multiple-choice format

There is advice on filling in the multiple-choice answer sheets on page 2 of the answer sheet booklet. Read through this advice with your child before you begin. Make sure that they understand what they need to do before they begin a paper, and that they are filling in the answer sheet which matches the paper they are attempting.

How to set the practice papers

- Do the practice papers at a time when your child usually works well. This might be a weekday after school, or at the weekend. This will help them work to the best of their abilities.
- As you get closer to the actual test, it is a good idea to sit some practice papers at the same time of day as the real thing — that way, your child will be used to the routine and there shouldn't be any surprises.
- Your child should attempt the practice paper at a clear table in a quiet area, free from distractions and interruptions.
- They'll need a sharp pencil, an eraser and a pencil sharpener.
- You can play the online audio to mimic real exam conditions. The audio runs through the instructions found on the front of the practice paper, and will give your child information about timings.
- If you're not using the online audio instructions, read out the instructions on the front of the practice paper before your child begins. Make sure that they understand what they have to do. Position your child so they can see a watch or clock so that they can keep track of the time they have left.
- Time the test strictly. If they haven't finished the paper in the time allowed, you could draw a line under the last question they answered within the time limit so you know to give marks up to that point. You can then time them to see how long it takes them to finish the paper. This will allow you to monitor the speed your child is working at.
- Encourage them to read over their answers if they finish within the time limit, but don't give them extra time to do this.
- Mark their test using the answers in the separate answer booklet.

Marking the practice papers

You should give one mark for each correct answer your child gave within the time limit, then work out the total score. It's really important to go through any wrong answers with your child — use the explanations in the answer book to show them how to find the right answer.

The pass mark will vary from school to school and year to year. It's common practice for your child's 'raw score' (i.e. the actual number of questions they answered correctly) to be converted into a 'standardised score'. This helps to make the results fairer by taking your child's age into account, as well as bringing scores for different papers in line with each other. As such, there is no number of correct answers that will guarantee a pass, but for these practice papers, we suggest that your child aims for a score of 85% or more.

Your child's score might help you pinpoint specific skills that they need to practise. For example, if your child scored 60%, got nearly all the questions right, but didn't finish the test, they need to work faster. We have given some advice to help you increase your child's speed on p.6.

If they scored 60%, got to the end, but got 40% of the questions wrong, they need to brush up on their accuracy. You can follow this up with some more practice in the areas they struggled with, then set another practice test.

Improving Your Child's Score

For your child to do well in their 11+, they'll need to work quickly and avoid making mistakes. Here's some advice to help improve your child's score and test technique.

Start by working on accuracy...

When your child is just starting out, it's a good idea to focus on their accuracy and understanding, rather than speed. You can work on their speed when they're a bit more confident.

Once your child has finished a paper and you've marked it, you should go over the questions they got wrong, so they know how they should have answered them. You could even come back to these trickier questions at a later date to make sure they can still get them right.

...then work on speed

In the real 11+ test, children are deliberately put under time pressure. This helps schools distinguish between good candidates and the best ones. The faster your child is, the more questions they'll answer. Once your child can accurately answer 11+ questions, use these tips to help them improve their speed:

- Find out the timings of the real test — how long your child will have, and how many questions they'll have to answer. When they're practising, give them slightly less time than this to do the same number of questions.
- Encourage your child only to check their answers if they have time at the end of the test.
- You could introduce games to get them working faster — try using a stopwatch to time a set of questions, and get your child to ring a bell or shout when they've finished them.
- For comprehension questions, it's important that your child can read the text quickly. Encourage them to read the text first, then look at the questions — remind them that they can look back at the text as many times as they like when answering the questions.

In the run-up to the test, start working on test technique

Your child will score better on the 11+ if they improve their test technique. Good test technique is also important for their SATs, and other exams later in their education. When they start working through assessment papers, remind them to do the following things:

- Read the front of the paper and enter the correct information on it.
- Skip any questions that are really difficult, or which are taking a long time — they can come back to them if there's time at the end.
- If they can't do a question and they're running out of time, make a sensible guess. For multiple-choice questions, they may be able to rule out one or two options that definitely aren't correct, which gives a better chance of guessing which of the remaining ones is right.

If your child's test is in multiple-choice format, there are some other specific techniques to practise:

- Marking the correct box neatly and quickly using a horizontal line.
- Making sure they mark the answer in the correct box, especially if they skip a question.
- If they don't finish the paper, filling in the rest of the answers randomly.

When your child does a practice paper, they should work in silence and without help. Try to make their experience as close to the real test as possible.

What to Expect on Test Day

The test day and the time before you get the results can be just as stressful for you as for your child. Here are some tips about how to reduce this stress, and how to cope with the waiting period.

Facing the test

Make sure you and your child are fully prepared for the day of the test. You need to know:

- Where the test is and how you're going to get there (parking may be difficult).
- What time the test starts and what time you need to arrive by.
- What they'll need to take (pencils, etc.) or whether everything is provided for them.

Make sure your child is as relaxed as possible the night before the test, and that they get a good night's sleep. A healthy evening meal and breakfast before the test will also help put your child in the right frame of mind to tackle the test. It's also a good idea to talk them through the arrangements for the day so they know what will happen.

After the test, plan an outing or a treat which will take your child's (and your) mind off the test. Even if your child is still preparing for other 11+ tests, they'll need a break.

- There's usually a retest day for children who are ill on the day of the test. Check with the school in advance, and let the test centre know as soon as possible if you can't make it to the test.
- If you think there are circumstances that have affected your child's performance in the test, gather evidence of this as soon as possible (e.g. a doctor's note or school marks that have dipped). Once you've got the results it'll be too late.

After the 11+

Make a plan for the time between the last of your child's tests and the day you get their results — this wait can be very stressful.

If you're going to reward your child for their hard work preparing for the 11+, you might want to do it now. If they're rewarded for their effort and hard work, they'll realise that they've achieved something, even if their results aren't what they hoped for.

Remind your child that you are proud of them no matter what the outcome, and try not to build up results day as too big a deal. If your child is unsuccessful, then it's not the end of the world. If your child does gain a grammar school place, then make sure they're aware that some of their classmates might not have done, and may need a friend to help make them feel better.

If you feel there is good reason, then this is also a good time to research the appeals process for the schools you've applied to. Some parents choose to appeal the admission decision if their child isn't offered a place.

Make sure you have an alternative plan

For some grammar schools, there can be several applicants for each available place. Even if your child scores highly on the test, it may still not be enough to gain a place at the school. You should put at least one non-selective school on your secondary school application form — it's a good idea to have visited these schools, so your child knows what to expect if they aren't offered a grammar school place.

It's important that your child doesn't feel like a failure if they don't get into a grammar school — there are many excellent comprehensive schools where your child can be happy and successful. Remember that school is what you make it, and a positive response to not gaining a grammar school place is key to this.